Kathleen McConnell Fad
James E. Gilliam

The **New Teacher's** Survival Guide

Stuff That Works

Originally published as *Putting It Together*,
Copyright 1996 by Kathleen McConnell Fad and James E. Gilliam

Copyright 2000 by Kathleen McConnell Fad and James E. Gilliam

05   04   03   02   6   5   4   3

Edited by Raven Moore
Text layout by Susan Fogo
Cover design by Becky Malone
Cover photo © 2000 PhotoDisc, Inc.

ISBN# 1-57035-322-0

Printed in the United States of America
Published and Distributed by:

SOPRIS
WEST

4093 Specialty Place   Longmont, CO 80504   (303) 651-2829   www.sopriswest.com

90PASS/GOR/8-02/1.5M/561

dedication

about the authors

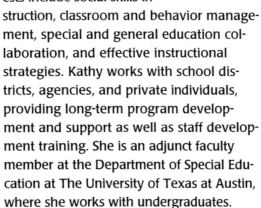

Dr. Kathleen McConnell Fad is an education consultant living in Austin, Texas. Kathy's professional interests include social skills instruction, classroom and behavior management, special and general education collaboration, and effective instructional strategies. Kathy works with school districts, agencies, and private individuals, providing long-term program development and support as well as staff development training. She is an adjunct faculty member at the Department of Special Education at The University of Texas at Austin, where she works with undergraduates.

Kathy enjoys spending time with her children, extended family, and friends. She also enjoys traveling, gardening, water sports, and perfecting her Spanish language skills.

Dr. James E. Gilliam is an associate professor at The University of Texas at Austin. Jim has written numerous journal articles and tests, most recently a rating scale for predicting students' success in general education environments. In addition to his teaching and research, Jim also coordinates a statewide conference on children with emotional/behavioral disorders, held each year in Austin, Texas. He serves as a consultant to several school districts and works closely with special education directors and consultants in the areas of behavioral disorders and autism.

Jim recently took a leave of absence from his faculty position to take an extended trip across the country. In addition to travel, he enjoys working on his computers and watching sports events.

table of contents

Introduction . . . 1

Establishing a Positive Climate

1 Be an Effective Communicator . . . 5

2 Create a Community in Your Classroom . . . 23

3 Use Plenty of Positive Reinforcement . . . 47

4 Encourage Cooperation and Compliance . . . 71

5 Teach Positive Social Skills . . . 87

Planning for Positive Behavior

6 Define Your Expectations and Establish Clear Rules . . . 105

7 Set up a "User-Friendly" System of Consequences . . . 141

8 Monitor Behavior Simply and Efficiently . . . 161

9 Take a Time-Out When Someone Needs a Breather . . . 181

10 Predict, Avoid, and Manage Crises . . . 195

Effective Classroom Management and Instruction

11 Put Together a Management System . . . 219

12 Individualize to Meet Students' Needs . . . 241

13 Use Cooperative Learning Structures . . . 259

14 Motivate Students to Learn . . . 275

15 Help Students Generalize Their Skills . . . 291

References . . . 309

Recommended Resources . . . 311

introduction

The New Teacher's Survival Guide was written for elementary and secondary teachers (both general and special education), student teachers and interns, and university instructors who teach courses in instructional methods or classroom organization and management. The book describes positive, practical approaches to instruction and management, and offers many supplemental resources such as sample letters, checklists, planning forms, definitions, guidelines, and activities. These tools (which appear at the end of each chapter) will make implementation of the ideas easy and fun; feel free to photocopy or adapt them to use with your students.

The New Teacher's Survival Guide will be a welcome addition to any teacher's library and is an excellent basis for preservice as well as inservice training. With increasingly challenging populations of students to teach, teachers will enjoy the clear, systematic, proactive approach of *The New Teacher's Survival Guide.* You will learn to connect with students through teamwork, a positive spirit, and effective application of ideas that work.

PART ONE

Establishing a Positive Climate

be an effective communicator

Without effective communication, teachers and students are unlikely to work together successfully.

Today's students often have problems relating to adults. The first step toward building good relationships is to establish or to improve communication. Effective communication will lead to a beneficial exchange of ideas and information.

Chapter 1

What to Do and How to Do it

1 Treat your students with respect.

Listen to them. Many students today have no one to listen to their hopes, dreams, or troubles. With the increasing number of families in which a single parent or both parents work, students often do not have an adult available with whom to share information and to whom they can look for guidance. Whether teachers like it or not, they may often be the most important adults in

students' lives, and the only adult confidants students have.

Maintain confidentiality (unless you are limited by legal or moral guidelines). It is neither professional nor ethical to violate students' trust by sharing their confidential information with others. If students find out that you have discussed their personal business with others (and they probably will find out eventually), you will have lost their trust forever. It will also be more difficult for them to trust other adults.

Set the parameters and explain to students your ethical obligations in sensitive situations. For example, confidential records such as special education records or health-related information will remain confidential. However, if a student shares information regarding abuse or potential suicide, teachers are legally and ethically obligated to contact appropriate authorities. Each school district will be bound by state and local guidelines, and each teacher should become familiar with the rules.

It is difficult to get to know or trust people when you don't even know their names. This is a very basic introductory activity which can be modified and adapted to fit almost any age range or group size.

- As soon as possible (the first day of school or of the new semester), assign each student to a partner.
- Ask the students to introduce themselves to their partners.
- Ask students to tell their partners something about their names. The details can vary, depending on students' ages, levels of communication, familiarity with each other, etc. Some ideas include:
  - Whom they're named for
  - The ethnic origins of their names
  - What each name means in its original language
  - Whether they like their names
  - What their nicknames are
- After each pair has exchanged names, they can share with another pair, introduce their partners to the whole class, or change to new partners.

the name game

2 Exchange information with students.

Begin by learning their names. Start the academic year by telling students your name and by learning their names as quickly as possible. Then be sure they know the names of their classmates. It's amazing how many students don't know the names of people in their classes. It's very basic information, and necessary for friendly communication. For secondary teachers who see as many as 120 students each day, it may be necessary to use name tags, name cards, or seating charts at first. You may also want to begin with a low-key group activity like the Name Game.

Tell them about yourself, then invite them to share with you. One way to initiate communication is to share some basic information with your students, so they start to connect with and care about you. Then, give them a chance to talk. Students who are not used to talking to teachers may find it very difficult to share information about themselves. However, some non-intrusive questions about hobbies, brothers and sisters, favorite foods, etc. can get things started. Once a dialogue has started, you can get a sense of how comfortable you and your students are with friendly conversations, and you can build on the basic information. Here are some ideas for sharing:

- Invite one of your family members to have lunch with your class at school (your mother, father, spouse, child, etc.).
- Create a bulletin board by displaying pictures of students when they were babies or toddlers. Then let students guess who's who.
- Show them pictures of you when you were younger.
- Call their parents and say "hello." Don't wait until there's a problem.
- Tell them about your hobbies. Share pictures of your sports car or tell them about your travels.
- Eat lunch with them and promise not to talk about school.
- Mail notes or postcards to them at home so they get some mail of their own. Write something about your activities. Give them each a stamped postcard to send to you.
- Tell them about your pets. Ask about their pets. Share pictures.

- Have theme days—50s Day, Hat Day, Hippie Day, etc. Wear something of yours that is old and/or special.

3 Speak (or at least understand) your students' language.

Learn their jargon. Understanding the language that adolescents and teenagers use is not easy. Their colloquialisms and slang are subject to rapid change. Most students do not expect (or appreciate) adults who try to be just like them, but making an attempt to learn the basics will increase your understanding of the unspoken rules governing social interactions. You don't have to talk like the kids, but it's helpful to be able to understand what they're saying.

"In good conversation, parties don't speak to the words, but to the meanings of each other."   Emerson

---

Pay attention to their music. Music has become an important medium for transmitting the culture of our young people. Music videos on television, portable CD technology, radios, and live concerts have made music a universal language. You can learn a lot about the latest hairstyles, fashion trends, and mannerisms when you become familiar with contemporary music. By listening to

some of the lyrics, you may also gain an understanding of the values, issues, and concerns of young people. Many adults are concerned about the behaviors that popular music endorses. It is wise to know what influences are operating on your students.

4 Give directions in a way that students understand.

Be clear about what you want them to do. Using a slow, structured approach when giving directions may seem like a waste of time. However, many teachers spend a lot more time answering questions and correcting mistakes because they rush through directions, or because they fail to provide an explanation, assuming that students know what they mean. Try this structured format for giving directions:

- Stand quietly and wait for attention. You may wish to use a quiet signal. Signals cut down on verbal interactions and

they don't interrupt your teaching. The quieter the signal, the better. Try these:

- A peace sign
- An "OK" sign
- A picture
- Holding up a "STOP" sign
- A finger to your lips to signal "shh"
- Color signals (like red for stop, yellow for a warning, and green when everything is OK)
- Flashing the room lights off and on
- A silent cheer
- A high five
- Thumbs up or down
- "The Look" (translation: settle down **now**)

- Use one short sentence to cue them to listen. Then tell them why it is important to listen.

"I am going to tell you how to get ready for your pop quiz. It is important that you listen carefully, because I will not repeat the directions once the quiz has begun."

- Try not to present more than two or three steps at once when giving directions. Use cue words like "first," "second," "next," "last," etc. Model by providing a sample on the blackboard or overhead, or by demonstrating.

"First, put your heading on your paper."
"Second, fold your paper in half."

(Demonstrate)
"Third, put your pencil and paper down and look at me."

- Ask students to repeat the directions to a partner.

    "Turn to the person next to you and tell him/her the directions. Answer any questions your partner may have."

- Allow students to ask questions.

    If the questions are relevant, answer them.

- Tell the students to begin their assignment.

- Do not repeat the directions once students have begun the assignment. If students have questions, they may ask their partners. If they still have questions, they may then ask you, but you should answer specific questions only.

Always use concrete examples. If possible, demonstrate what you want your students to do. Not everyone can follow oral directions. Many students, especially those with attention or concentration problems, can do well if they have a pattern to follow or a completed example to use as a model for their own work. Save copies of papers, projects, and other products, so that the next time you give a similar assignment you can provide students with a concrete example.

5 Be sure you're clear about a situation before you act.

Check your perceptions. Different individuals perceive situations differently. Sometimes we make very rapid judgments about people's motives, feelings, and levels of understanding. For example, when faced with a rude or defiant student, a teacher may automatically assume that the student is confident and secure, when in fact that student may be fearful and anxious. Teachers may also fail to recognize sad and depressed students, especially when they seem angry and hostile instead of withdrawn and passive. If you are trying to clarify a student's feelings about an issue, you can always use a One-Minute Hall Conference. This strategy can give you helpful

information for the moment, then you can arrange a more in-depth conference if you think it is necessary.

Don't overreact because of your own feelings. There are many reasons why we behave the way that we do. When we are stressed, tired, nervous, ill, or worried, we may overreact to individuals and situations. We may also reflect back to students the feelings that they are sharing. For example, when a student is angry and threatening, he/she may provoke a response from a teacher that is angry and threatening. Likewise, if a student is sarcastic, a teacher may also be tempted to use sarcasm, especially if the teacher is tired. It is important to maintain some separation from students' feelings and not move quickly into an extreme reaction. One strategy that may help is to "buy"

- Ask the student if he/she would like to join you in the hall.
- Tell the student that you would like to check out your perceptions. Try saying something like, "It seems to me that you might be feeling . . . I just wanted to make sure I am not misunderstanding things. Would you like to talk to me about what is going on?"
- If the student wants to talk, listen and ask clarifying questions.
- Then ask whether the student would like to set up a longer, more in-depth conference at another time.
- Finish with, "Is there anything else that I can do to help you?"

one-minute hall conference

yourself some time by postponing your own reaction. This helps everyone to save face, and may prevent a situation from escalating out of control. Use some of these strategies when you need to buy time:

- Tell the student that you have another obligation and can consider the problem at lunch (or after school or before school).

- Tell the student that you are not sure of the rules and must check with someone else.

- Tell the student that you have not heard from everyone yet and must listen to everyone involved.

- Tell the student that you forgot something and must find it before you make a decision.

- Ask the student if he/she would like a cold drink before beginning the discussion.

- Tell the student that you have to go to the bathroom before sitting down to talk.

- Ask the student to write down his/her concerns.

Don't assume that you can read someone's mind. We often *think* that we know what is happening, even when we don't. Teachers, in particular, are often empathetic and understanding individuals. Because of

these qualities and because they often build very close relationships with students, teachers may begin to make inaccurate assumptions about situations and individuals. Before you react to a student's behavior, take the time to ask what is going on; you may be getting only one point of view. There's an old saying that bears remembering when dealing with young people: "Just because you think it doesn't make it true." Always check things out—-with parents, with other teachers, and with students. If you want to know why something is happening, stop talking and listen.

❻ Give and receive feedback.

Provide correction, then offer solutions. Although teaching will always require some constructive criticism, negative information by itself is limited in its usefulness. It points out what not to do, but does not teach students what they should do instead. When providing corrective feedback, try to explain specifically what was done correctly

and what was not, then suggest ways to improve performance. Also remember to praise approximations of the desired behavior or performance. As the student improves, it is essential that he/she be given lots of praise, and lots of suggestions for how to do even better. By using praise and other positive reinforcement strategies, you can build confidence, acknowledge progress, and establish a positive classroom atmosphere.

When giving a student feedback, keep in mind that almost no one wants to hear that he/she has done something wrong. Bob Algozzine (1993) suggested a technique he called a "Criticism Sandwich" that can be used with students. It sandwiches the criticism between two layers of praise:

- First, praise the student on one part of the assignment or one aspect of the behavior.

- Then, give the constructive criticism on the part(s) that he/she needs to complete, correct, delete, or modify.

- Finally, end with another positive comment, perhaps something encouraging like, "Stay with it. You're really making progress."

Try to remain encouraging. Some teachers have not yet realized how powerful positive messages are and how devastating public criticism can be. Whenever you give feedback, do it in a way that you yourself might like. Consider whether the feedback should be given publicly or privately. When using a student's work as a positive example, share the student's name with the class (with his/her permission). When pointing out problems or negative qualities, present students' work anonymously (erase the name), try to use an example from another class, make up a hypothetical student, or present one of last year's products.

Find out how well you communicate. Teachers (understandably) focus on how well their students do things. Sometimes, it's a good idea to get students' feedback on how well teachers do things. Form 1 (at the end of this chapter) is a quick and easy evaluation form that you can use to collect information about your own communication skills. You may wish to modify this procedure by using pictures or symbols, or reading the questions orally if you're working with very young children or with non-readers.

7 Learn to be comfortable saying "no."

When it's necessary, say "no" clearly and directly. It is sometimes very unpleasant and difficult to hear the word "no" when you're asking for something. For some people, telling someone "no" is just as difficult. Teachers may have a hard time

telling students they can't have or do something, because the students' reactions can be negative, intimidating, frightening, or otherwise unpleasant. Nevertheless, it may be better to "bite the bullet" and tell a student "no" immediately and directly, rather than opening the door for students' bargaining, wheedling, or cajoling. Most students will (eventually) appreciate your honesty and directness. Here are some ideas for how to say "no:"

● Make eye contact when you say "no."
● Be clear and direct.
● Express the other person's request, and explain how it conflicts with your goal.
● Suggest other options.
● Tell the truth.

After you have said "no," be consistent. Teachers who are clear about their expectations and who respond consistently to students' behavior will set up a predictable environment for their students. When an environment is predictable, students know what to expect in most situations and under most circumstances. Students can then make informed decisions about their own behavior, based on the expected outcomes. There will always be exceptions to every rule or situation, but a teacher's consistent behavior is likely to foster students' consistent behavior. If you don't mean it, don't say it. If you say you're going to do it, do it.

8 Include parents in the communication loop.

Find an easy, convenient way to communicate. All too often, misunderstandings occur between family members and educators because of infrequent or unclear communication. Because teachers are always very busy, it is important to find ways to communicate that are easy and convenient to use. One way to save time is to have a form available to use for notes home. (Form 2 is a sample to get you started.) Keep several blank copies of a form in your desk, or have a template form on your computer. This can save time and make regular communication simpler for everyone. Another

strategy is to use a spiral notebook that goes back and forth from school to home in the student's notebook or backpack. In this way, teachers and parents can conduct an ongoing dialogue and discuss problems, upcoming events, assignments, and concerns.

Require students to use a monitoring form. While Form 2 or the spiral notebook will allow for communication on almost any topic, you may sometimes want to monitor specific issues with a student. Keeping up with these situations on a regular basis can prevent things from sliding out of control before anyone is aware of what is happening. There are many forms available to monitor students' behavior, academic performance,

academic responsibilities, and attendance. These forms are most helpful when they are used daily, and when students are required to obtain parents' signatures on them. You can use positive reinforcement to teach and encourage students to return the forms, which can then be kept for documentation. The forms are a way of alerting parents and teachers to potential problems, or to problematic situations that are still in their early stages. We have included two samples (Forms 3 and 4), both from *The Tough Kid Tool Box* by Jenson, Rhode, and Reavis (1994). Form 3 is meant for monitoring academic performance, and Form 4 is for monitoring behavior. (For more information on behavior monitoring, see Chapter 8.)

Forms
for
Chapter

1

form 1 Communication Rating Scale

Please do not write your name on this paper.

Please rate my performance on the items below according to this scale:	1 = Never 2 = Usually 3 = Always
1. I speak clearly. You can understand my words.	_____
2. I talk at a good pace for learning (not too slow, not too fast).	_____
3. When I teach a new skill, I give clear explanations.	_____
4. I allow enough time for questions.	_____
5. I give enough examples of the new ideas I present.	_____
6. When I give directions, I explain them clearly and go slowly enough.	_____
7. When I change topics or activities, I allow enough time for you to get ready.	_____
8. I make it clear how the information I'm giving is meaningful or useful to you.	_____
9. I have about the right number of activities planned for each class period (not too many, not too few).	_____
10. My written instructions/explanations are clear and understandable.	_____
11. When we have class discussions, you can follow what we're talking about.	_____

Comments:

form 2 Home Note

Note From School to Home

Date:

To:

From:

Signature:

Reply From Home

Signature: Date:

form 3 Information Note–Academic Performance

Student Name:_____ Date/Week of: _____Phone: _____

Period/Class	Teacher's Initials	Class Performance (circle one)	Assigned Homework	Upcoming Tests	Missing Work
		G Great A Average U Unsatisfactory			
		G Great A Average U Unsatisfactory			
		G Great A Average U Unsatisfactory			
		G Great A Average U Unsatisfactory			
		G Great A Average U Unsatisfactory			
		G Great A Average U Unsatisfactory			
		G Great A Average U Unsatisfactory			

Comments:

Counselor's Signature: Parent's Signature:

Reprinted with permission from Jenson, W.R., Rhode, G., & Reavis, H.K. (1994). *The tough kid tool box*. Longmont, CO: Sopris West.

form 4 Information Note–Behavior

Name: _____ Date/Week of: _____

Select a few specific behaviors you want to monitor for the student, then rate the student according to how well he/she exhibits each one.

Behavior(s)	Teacher's Initials	MON	TUE	WED	THUR	FRI
Parent's Initials						

Rating Scale: Unsatisfactory = 1   Average = 2   Great = 3

Comments:

Teacher's Phone: Parent's Phone:

Reprinted with permission from Jenson, W.R., Rhode, G., & Reavis, H.K. (1994). *The tough kid tool box.* Longmont, CO: Sopris West.

create a community in your classroom

A community is a group of individuals who are unified by a common purpose and by common interests. Creating a community in the classroom can foster students' interdependence and cooperation.

For many young people whose families and neighborhoods are in disarray, the most important community to which they belong is their school. Their desire for a sense of belonging and their search for role models, if not met in their school, may be met by gangs or by other anti-social groups. Students, teachers, and administrators share a common goal: the cultivation of learning. They can help each other by establishing an atmosphere of cooperation, mutual respect, and pursuit of the common good of the group.

Chapter 2

What to Do and How to Do it

1 Share with students the importance of an education.

Show them why they should want an education. It is never too soon to talk about the importance of an education. For many students, school may be the only place in their environment where discussions occur about the value of education.

Teachers are in an excellent position to encourage young people with their own excitement for learning and enthusiasm for education, or to discourage students by expressing a dislike for their jobs and a cynicism about education. Of course, any discussion of the value of education must match its audience. A kindergarten teacher will not discuss education in the same language or framework as will a secondary

school teacher. There are numerous ways to share a belief in the value of education and the positive aspects of school:

- Invite individuals from the community to speak to your students about what education has meant to them. Make sure you include individuals whose ethnic backgrounds and cultural experiences are similar to those of your students.

- Use statistics that compare lifetime earnings with and without a high school or college education as part of a lesson in math or social studies.

- Ask your students' parents and siblings to come to school and tell stories about their favorite teachers.

- Set up cross-age tutoring situations so that younger students have older role models.

- Find stories in the media about well-known, successful individuals who value education.

- Take students on field trips to visit special high schools, local colleges, universities, or vocational schools.

- Visit local businesses so that students can get ideas about job opportunities.

- Read want ads in the newspaper. Compare wages and salaries of various jobs.

- Share your own experiences in obtaining an education and deciding to become a teacher.

- Work with students to enter academic contests, find scholarships, and network with businesses and learning institutions.

- Find literature that stresses the positive outcomes available through education, and use it as teaching content.

- Set up pen pal or computer network arrangements in which students can find partners who are role models for staying in school.

- If students are determined to drop out of school, encourage them to explore nontraditional alternative learning options.

- Communicate with parents and other family members. Try to get them into the building. Start with something fun, like a breakfast or lunch visit that will encourage positive feelings about school.

- Share positive information with families. Establish good working relationships, so that students hear good things about school from the people at home.

- Somewhere in your classroom, hang up your diplomas, graduation pictures, certificates and honors, etc. Let students see how much you value your own education.

Help them see the relevance of what they are learning. Many of us recall learning things in school that seemed totally irrelevant and useless. Today's students are no different. It is important to share with students the purpose of what you are asking them to do. Just because they think that something is irrelevant does not mean that it is; however, the older the students, the more important it is to address the relevance of activities and lessons. It is also helpful to tie in classroom learning with practical applications in the world outside school. Use real life examples when teaching concepts or presenting information, and present application problems (homework assignments) that are rooted in practical experiences.

2 Encourage a team spirit in your classroom.

Begin to teach specific skills required for group functioning. Throughout the course of an academic year, you will structure numerous opportunities to learn. Many

As a reward, let one student be the "teacher for the day." While acting as teacher, the lucky student gets to sit at the teacher's desk, eat lunch with other teachers, and have a "planning time" activity of his/her choice.

teacher for the day

tasks will require students to act independently. It is helpful, though, to also design and implement cooperative activities that require students to depend on each other. Cooperative activities designed for academic content areas will be described in more detail in Chapter 13; however, they cannot be implemented successfully unless students are first taught interaction skills. For students whose only priority so far has been meeting their personal needs, teamwork may require a shift in thinking and in behavior. Try the following approach for teaching teamwork to your students: (1) Identify the specific teamwork skills your students are lacking (a list is given here to help you), (2) Prioritize them in order of most to least important, and (3) Design team-building activities that focus on each required skill. (You can find more on this subject in Chapter 13.) Some skills required for successful teamwork are:

- Attending

  - Listening
  - Staying with your group
  - Establishing eye contact
  - Smiling/head nodding
  - Facing group members/leaning toward group

- Showing Interest

  - Taking turns/sharing
  - Making supportive/positive comments

  - Asking for clarification
  - Accepting others' ideas and suggestions/complimenting
  - Making positive statements/giving feedback

- Demonstrating Involvement

  - Sharing feelings/making "I feel" statements
  - Answering questions
  - Expressing concern and interest about others
  - Requesting more information
  - Volunteering to do more

Make interdependence among your students a priority. The suggestion that teachers endeavor to build a community spirit will likely elicit concern about how this non-academic goal can be accomplished in an environment where time is limited and where academic content and test scores are highly valued. With those concerns in mind, any activities undertaken to foster teamwork within a class should be based on a firm belief that they are necessary and important. The relationships among individuals in the classroom must be a priority for you, and their value must be clearly understood if team-building efforts are to be successful. Read the following section for some simple ways to begin to improve teamwork in your class.

3 Have fun with your students.

Start with a scavenger hunt. Some of the most effective team-building activities are those that do not involve academic tasks. There are many ways to structure situations so that students work together in non-threatening, enjoyable ways. The focus at the beginning is not on content; it is on the *process* of working together. Students who don't know each other very well, or who are diverse ethnically and culturally, still have common interests and characteristics. Use a scavenger hunt to emphasize things that students have in common and to allow them to move around and talk to each other. Form 5 is a sample; you can adjust the number and content of items to fit your particular class.

Try a fun puzzle or game. Students who are not strong in academic areas may have other skills. Structuring thinking and discussion activities allows them to work together with others, perhaps contributing information that no one else knows. The activity on Form 6 is one way to start. Assign students to groups of three or four. Give one copy of the paper to each group. Set a timer for five to ten minutes, and encourage students to help each other. Reinforce the groups who get a certain percentage correct, who involve everyone in the group, who help each other, or who meet any other criteria you choose. The same structure can be used for the Out of This World activity (Form 7).

There are many other wonderful sources of puzzles and activities to help build teams. One is *101 Games for Groups* by Ashton and Varga (1993) and another is Gardner's *Perplexing Puzzles and Tantalizing Teasers* (1988). These and other game ideas are available both through educational publishers and in your local bookstores.

4 Encourage the continuing use of positive group behaviors.

Reward students for actions that benefit the group. After you have begun to teach skills that improve group interdependence and teamwork in your classroom, it is important to reinforce students

S tart a "Secret Friends" program in your school. Teachers select students who need a secret friend and, without revealing their identities, share special goodies with those students. Birthday cards, encouraging notes, rewards for special accomplishments, and treats will all help their secret friends feel special.

secret friends

for demonstrating those skills. Just as with any other desirable behaviors, group interaction skills must be reinforced in order to be strengthened and maintained. Decide on some simple ways to praise and reward your students when you see them using their group skills. (Specific details for effective use of positive reinforcement are presented in Chapter 3.)

Emphasize social, as well as academic, skills in your teaching. In addition to improving cooperative skills through systematic, consistent positive reinforcement, take advantage of other opportunities to foster positive teamwork in the classroom. There are numerous opportunities throughout the school year to focus on cooperative interpersonal skills. Following are some ways to continue team building in your classroom and to combine it with your academic teaching. Try these tactics:

- Let the students choose a team name and symbol. With all of the current gang activity, it is probably best to limit

use of sports team logos and colors, or hand signs. Stick to categories like ocean animals, birds, dinosaurs, computer terms, countries, horses, famous authors, types of airplanes, etc.

- Take advantage of incidental teaching opportunities to emphasize the sharing of ideas and materials.

- Find media examples of strong cooperative relationships.

- Assign grades both for academic performance and for social competencies.

- Establish peer tutoring programs in your class, or cross-age peer tutoring with other classes.

- Pair students together to be homework buddies or reading partners.

- Focus on students' improvement rather than on their overall performance.

- Change small groups regularly so that everyone gets to know everyone else.

- Use games and sports. Try to play a variety of sports, including ones that students may not have learned, like ping pong, volleyball, golf (use a public course), bowling, Frisbee® golf, etc. Emphasize teamwork and fun, not competition.

5 Help your students connect to their communities.

Find out how much they know. Many students are not involved in their communities. They do not have positive relationships with people in their neighborhoods, especially people who are older or younger than themselves. Before beginning to encourage community involvement, it may be helpful to find out how much your students know about their immediate neighborhood and larger community. A quick and easy ques-

tionnaire (like Form 8) can help you evaluate their level of knowledge.

Focus some of your instruction on the community. For most of us, it is difficult to care about something we know nothing about and/or have never experienced. Many students have similar attitudes about their communities. Fortunately, there are many ways to teach students about where they live and the people among whom they live. Hopefully, some of the information students gain will encourage them to become more involved in their community and to build a sense of commitment to it. An interdisciplinary unit of instruction that integrates geography, math, social studies, and language arts activities can be an enjoyable way for students and teachers to learn about their community together. For example, a unit on recycling might include examining areas of the world where resources are scarce, computing the projected costs of environmental cleanup, debating pros and cons of conservation laws, and writing a research paper on a current legal issue. Other activities are suggested here that can be used as individualized learning opportunities:

- Teach a short unit on maps and map-making that uses each student's own street, neighborhood, town, and state as the assigned topics.

- Locate and describe all of the parks and recreation areas in the community; include a list of the activities available in each, and a map showing their locations.

- Have students list their hobbies or interests. Then use the telephone book and newspaper to identify all of the businesses and groups devoted to each interest.

- Invite community members to visit who have unique and interesting experiences to share. Focusing on specific cultures, ethnic groups, and age groups at various times might increase students' understanding of those different from themselves.

- Expose students to various activities in the arts, including art exhibits in banks and other businesses, art galleries and shops, theaters that have live performances, children's art activities in bookstores, music venues, etc. Find out performance schedules and costs.

- Locate opportunities for sports and other physical activities, including health clubs, public golf courses, tennis courts, lakes and creeks for fishing, etc.

- Have each student make a map of his/her street or his/her apartment building. Include house numbers and the names of people who live there. Many students may, for the first time, learn who their neighbors are.

- Teach students to use public transportation, including how to read and understand bus and train schedules. Practice with a field trip to someplace fun.

6 Work with your students to improve quality of life in the community.

Start a community service project.

Many students respond positively to volunteer opportunities. Working with your students on service projects can build a sense of common purpose and belonging. They may also form ties to those whom they meet during their work. Nursing homes, other classrooms in school, libraries, day care centers, and many other groups frequently welcome student volunteers. It is important that students keep their commitments when they volunteer, so plan ahead and don't take on more than you can accomplish.

Arrange some outdoor activities. Global
environmental issues are increasingly important in our world. Help your students relate to these issues on a personal level by teaching them to value and appreciate the outdoors. For students who live in cities or have not participated in outdoor activities,

expose them to opportunities to do so. Some ideas are provided here:

- Start seedlings, and teach students to transplant and nurture them until they are adult plants.

- Plant an outdoor garden. If you don't have much space, use pots and window boxes. Include vegetables, fruits, and flowers.

- Ask retirees or others in the community who are gardeners and may have time during the school day to share information with your students.

- Plan a thematic unit on endangered species of plants and animals. Write for information from environmental organizations, use media such as educational videotapes, and involve students in writing about problems and solutions.

- Visit local gardens, arboretums, and parks.

- Ask a local garden center to help you with advice, classes, discounted merchandise, etc.

- Raise plants and sell them to earn money for the next crop.

- Combine environmental topics with science, geography, and social studies units.

- Visit a ranch or farm if there are some close by. Give students an opportunity to discuss the lifestyle of farmers and ranchers.

- Set up a time for gardening once or twice per week, either at school or somewhere else in the community, like a nursing home or community garden.

- Visit grocery stores to compare varieties of produce. Integrate this with a math, science, or language arts assignment.

- Take your students fishing. Ask for help from local fishing enthusiasts (find a boat store or bait shop and ask for their assistance).

- Walk or jog with your students.

7 Build strong relationships with your students' families.

Start with a positive attitude. Some teachers, especially when working with difficult and challenging students, may find themselves in adversarial relationships with parents and other family members. These teachers might spend time and energy blaming their students' families for their students' "problems." There are, of course, some parents who are neglectful or abusive toward their children. There are also families who are hostile and uncooperative in their relationships with teachers and administrators. Nevertheless, until you are convinced otherwise, assume that most parents *do* care about their children and that they *are* interested in helping their children succeed. Begin with a positive attitude and expect the best!

Think about parents' experiences. Consider how your students' parents may have felt about school when they were young. If their experiences were negative and unsuccessful, they may have communicated their feelings to their children. In this case, you must focus as much on the students' families as on the students. There are many ways of improving school-family-community relationships:

- Say and do something positive. Send notes, cards, and letters through the mail to your students' homes. Make a positive phone call to every family.

- Make home visits. If you need an escort for neighborhoods that might be dangerous, find one, but make the effort to meet families in *their* environment, not yours. (Escorts may include one of your friends, your spouse, another teacher, an administrator, the parent of another student who lives nearby, or students and their friends.)

- Also invite families into your classroom. Ask for parent volunteers to help with special projects, or to plan a presentation or open house. Serve food.

- Share information with families. This includes asking them what they think. Parents usually know their children very well. Asking them for ideas may make a big difference in how effective your suggestions and strategies are.

- Share your knowledge in a non-threatening, positive way. No one likes to be talked down to or made to feel uneducated. If you have some suggestions that could be implemented at home, offer them in a way that is not accusatory or blaming, so that parents don't feel defensive.

- Talk to community leaders, including the clergy, the police, probation officers, judges, and business owners. The larger your network, the more options you have to expand programs and coordinate activities.

- Have some fun with parents. Invite them along on field trips, and into your class for holiday gatherings. Make it special when they come.

- Be honest. When there are problems, misunderstandings, or mistakes, try to be open and honest. If you need to apologize, do it.

Communicate, communicate, communicate. Sharing information with students' families is always a good idea. Some students are very skilled at telling one story to parents and another to teachers. It is usually a good idea to check things out with parents before believing everything that you hear. Chapter 1 mentioned ways to improve communication with parents through the use of home notes, but when in doubt, call parents and ask for (or share) accurate information.

Forms
for
Chapter
2

form 5 Scavenger Hunt

Obtain the signature (first name will do) of a person in the class for each of the following items. You may use a person's signature only once. You will have _____ minutes to collect as many signatures as you can.

_____ 1. Someone with the same eye color as you.

_____ 2. Someone who is the same height as you.

_____ 3. Someone who sleeps on a waterbed.

_____ 4. Someone who was born in the same month as you.

_____ 5. Someone who speaks another language in addition to English.

_____ 6. Someone with the same number of brothers and sisters as you.

_____ 7. Someone who uses the same brand of toothpaste as you.

_____ 8. Someone who knows how to play the guitar.

_____ 9. Someone who knows how to play chess.

_____ 10. Someone who wears the same size shoes as you.

_____ 11. Someone who has the same first initial as you.

_____ 12. Someone who knows how to sew.

_____ 13. Someone who eats the same brand of cereal as you.

_____ 14. Someone who likes to read the same kind of books as you.

_____ 15. Someone who likes to dance.

_____ 16. Someone who has a part-time job, either for money or just to help someone.

_____ 17. Someone who has traveled to another state.

_____ 18. Someone who can skateboard.

_____ 19. Someone who does volunteer work in school or in the community.

_____ 20. Someone who has the same color hair as you.

form 6 Something's Fishy

Many fish have names that describe how they look. With the other members of your group, look at each fish below, then match it with its correct name.

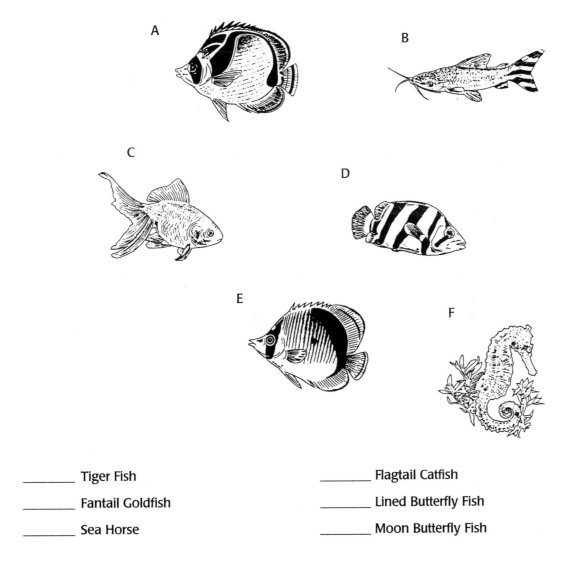

A

B

C

D

E

F

_____ Tiger Fish

_____ Fantail Goldfish

_____ Sea Horse

_____ Flagtail Catfish

_____ Lined Butterfly Fish

_____ Moon Butterfly Fish

form 6 Something's Fishy (Answer Key)

Many fish have names that describe how they look. With the other members of your group, look at each fish below, then match it with its correct name.

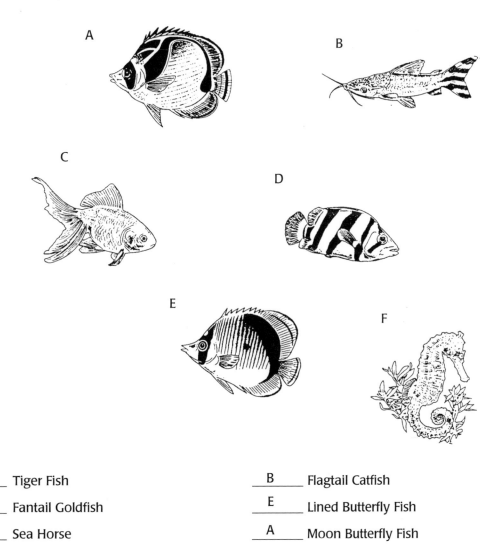

A

B

C

D

E

F

___D___   Tiger Fish   ___B___   Flagtail Catfish

___C___   Fantail Goldfish   ___E___   Lined Butterfly Fish

___F___   Sea Horse   ___A___   Moon Butterfly Fish

form 7 Out of This World

Work with your group to decide the correct answers to these questions about planets, stars, and space travel:

1. The sun is a

   A. star
   B. planet
   C. moon

2. The planets move around the sun along a path called

   A. an orbit
   B. a solar system
   C. an axis

3. Saturn's famous rings are made of billions of chunks of

   A. snow
   B. dust
   C. ice

4. The temperature of the inner core of the sun may reach as high as

   A. 35 thousand degrees
   B. 35 million degrees
   C. 35 hundred degrees

5. The largest planet is

   A. Venus
   B. Jupiter
   C. Pluto

6. How many moons does the Earth have?

   A. 22
   B. 0
   C. 1

form 7 Out of This World (Answer Key)

Work with your group to decide the correct answers to these questions about planets, stars, and space travel:

1. The sun is a

   (A.) star
   B. planet
   C. moon

2. The planets move around the sun along a path called

   (A.) an orbit
   B. a solar system
   C. an axis

3. Saturn's famous rings are made of billions of chunks of

   A. snow
   B. dust
   (C.) ice

4. The temperature of the inner core of the sun may reach as high as

   A. 35 thousand degrees
   (B.) 35 million degrees
   C. 35 hundred degrees

5. The largest planet is

   A. Venus
   (B.) Jupiter
   C. Pluto

6. How many moons does the Earth have?

   A. 22
   B. 0
   (C.) 1

form 8 Community Questionnaire

Fill in the blanks with as much information as you know. (Can be answered orally.)

1. Write your complete address, including city, state, and zip code:

    _____

    _____

    _____

2. Check these off once you can do each correctly:

    Find your country on a world map.
    Find your state on a United States map.
    Find your town or city on a state map.

3. Write down the names of three of your neighbors. Tell one thing you know about each of them.

    _____

    _____

    _____

4. Write the name and location of the closest (to your home):

    Hospital _____   Shopping center_____

    Post office _____   Veterinarian _____

    Gas station _____   Movie theater_____

    Nursing home or retirement center _____   Church or synagogue _____

    School (other than yours) _____

(cont'd)

form 8 (cont'd)

5. On your block or in your apartment building, are there any individuals who are over 60 years of age? If so, what are (were) their jobs? If they are retired, how do they spend their time now? _____

    _____

    _____

6. Are there people in your neighborhood who came to the United States from other countries?_____

    Could you find their "home" countries on a map? _____

    Do you know anything about their customs? _____

7. What holidays are celebrated in your community? _____

    _____

    Does your family celebrate some holidays that others do not?_____If so, which ones? _____

8. Who originally settled your town or city? _____

    Where were they from and why did they start the new community? _____

    _____

9. Are there places in your community where you can:

    See live plays?_____If so, where? _____

    Hear live music?_____If so, where?_____

    Watch live sports events?_____If so, where?_____

10. What is your favorite kind of food? _____

    Where can you get this food in your community? _____

11. What is one new thing you would like to learn about your community? _____

use plenty of positive reinforcement

One of the most effective ways to change students' behavior is to use positive reinforcement.

Using positive reinforcement consistently and effectively can result in significant improvement in student behavior. Positive reinforcement focuses on increasing and building behaviors rather than constantly trying to decrease or eliminate problems. The technique often results in long-term behavior changes.

Chapter 3

What to Do and How to Do it

1 Become familiar with the principles of positive reinforcement.

Begin by learning what positive reinforcement is. Positive reinforcement is a consequence that increases the occurrence of a behavior. The basic premise of reinforcement theory is that behavior is shaped or controlled by its immediate consequences. Not every behavior is completely controlled by its consequences, but a behavior can be more or less likely to occur again, depending on what happens after

the behavior. For example, if you go to a new grocery store to shop and find that prices are low and service is friendly, you may return to the store regularly. If your employer distributes cash bonuses for good attendance at work, you are more likely to go to work every day. On the other hand, if you arrange a fabulous anniversary dinner for your spouse and your efforts are ignored, you may not make special plans on your next anniversary. Positive reinforcement is a very effective strategy for teachers to use because it produces quick, noticeable results, it is a natural and constructive tech-

nique, and it emphasizes the increasing rather than the decreasing of behaviors.

Realize that "positive" is different for everyone. Keep in mind that we are all unique individuals and have individual preferences for activities, people, foods, drinks, attention, privileges, etc. Students have individual likes and dislikes. Some things that teachers assume are effective positive reinforcers can not only fail to increase desired behaviors; they may, in fact, decrease these behaviors. For example, when you compliment and praise Martin after he volunteers an answer, he may react with pride and pleasure. He will increase his volunteering in order to receive even more of your attention. Hannah, though, may be embarrassed and self-conscious when you compliment her contributions in class. For her, the unwanted attention from her teacher and peers is not a good experience. She will volunteer less often, preferring to respond only when asked a direct question. One way to determine whether a consequence is a positive reinforcer is to observe its effects. If a behavior occurs more often when you apply a certain consequence, the consequence is probably an effective positive reinforcer. If the behavior remains constant or decreases in frequency, the consequence may not be reinforcing.

2 Understand how positive reinforcement works.

Realize that positive reinforcement can increase all kinds of behaviors. Unfortunately, positive reinforcement may increase both desirable and undesirable behaviors. For example, in September, Lena begins a pattern of calling out questions without first raising her hand and waiting for teacher recognition. Her teacher, Mr. Sanford, responds to Lena's talking out by looking at her, answering her questions, and providing follow-up comments. By December, Lena is talking out in class all the time, and she frequently interrupts while Mr. Sanford is trying to present instruction. Unfortunately, without his knowing it, Mr. Sanford's responses to Lena have positively reinforced her undesirable and annoying behavior. Teacher attention often has a very strong positive reinforcement effect on a behavior, whether the behavior is desirable or not. It is important to note this fact, since sometimes teachers inadvertently and unknowingly positively reinforce undesirable behaviors without realizing the impact of their actions.

Follow some guidelines for maximum effectiveness. As with any intervention strategy, positive reinforcement sometimes works very quickly and very well. At other times, it seems to have no impact on students' behavior. Frequently, positive reinforcement is neither totally effective nor totally ineffective; rather, it seems to make a difference with only some students, or it works best when certain conditions are met, or it is effective only with particular types of behaviors. The effectiveness of positive reinforcement depends in part on the way that it is used. For maximum impact, positive reinforcement should have:

- Immediacy—Reinforcement should occur immediately following the behavior. The shorter the time between the behavior and the positive reinforcement, the more effective the reinforcement will be. This is especially true with young children.

Can't think of a reason to reinforce? What about these?

Compliment the student for:

- Being clean and well-groomed
- Smiling
- Offering to help someone
- Trying his/her best
- Thinking
- Taking turns
- Bringing materials to class
- Helping to collect papers

- Asking questions
- Being on time
- Raising his/her hand
- Doing a classroom chore without being asked
- Picking up trash off the floor
- Sharing
- Listening quietly

look for the positive

- Frequency—A behavior will increase more rapidly and more consistently if it is reinforced frequently. New behaviors that are being introduced should be reinforced after each occurrence. Intermittent reinforcement works well with established behaviors.

- Enthusiasm—When you present positive reinforcement to a student, look him/her in the eye, and be as enthusiastic as possible. Let students know that you value the particular behavior and that their behavior change is important and exciting. In the classroom, excitement is contagious.

- Significance—We have already discussed the fact that some reinforcement is meaningful and effective with particular individuals, and other reinforcement is not. Choosing reinforcers that are important, valuable, and significant to students is critical. If reinforcers are not significant to students, they will have little impact on behavior. Selection of reinforcers will be discussed elsewhere in this chapter.

- Consistency—Always be consistent in your delivery of reinforcers. Schedules for reinforcement should vary with the stage of instruction, the type of behavior targeted for change, and the age and skill level of students. However, when deciding on the reinforcement schedule, ensure ease and convenience of administration so that whatever the schedule, it is followed reliably.

- Variety and Novelty—There is not one reinforcer or group of reinforcers that will suit every individual or that will remain effective indefinitely. In fact, it is common for a reinforcer to work effectively for a period of time and then to lose its effectiveness, or to work beautifully with some students but not with others. Most people enjoy change. Students will lose interest when positive reinforcement lacks novelty and variety.

- Specificity—Positive reinforcement should follow, and be linked to, a specific, desirable behavior. For example, your compliments and praise should always include a description of a specific behavior. Vague, general reinforcement does not teach students exactly which behavior meets your criteria. This lack of understanding then makes it unlikely that the desired behavior will be repeated and mastered. Also, positive verbal praise should always accompany delivery of tangible reinforcers. That way, when you have phased out the tangibles, the social praise still remains as effective positive reinforcement.

3 Choose positive reinforcers that are most likely to work with students.

Ask students what they value. It is often difficult to predict what students enjoy, value, prefer, or find exciting. Rather than waste time guessing which reinforcers will work, ask you students directly. Some of the techniques and tools for determining students' preferences include questionnaires, menus, and surveys. They will help you find consequences that have enough appeal and value to warrant a behavior change. Using a reinforcement menu that includes several categories is also helpful. Categories can include tangible items, social reinforcers like attention and praise, and privileges or responsibilities. The various types of positive reinforcement can be used alone or in combination to produce the most effective results. We have included three sample tools (Forms 9-11) to assist you in selecting reinforcers for students.

Watch students for clues. Don't be discouraged by those students who fail to demonstrate interest or excitement in any reinforcers. There is *always* something that will be effective with a student, even though finding it can be a challenge. When asking students what is important to them doesn't get you a realistic or useful response, watch them carefully. Observe what they do, whom they do it with, how they spend free time, what activities they select when given choices, where they sit, what they eat and drink, where they ask to go, what books or magazines they read, what they wear, and anything else that may give you information about the consequences that influence their behavior. For students who are alienated, isolated, and unsocialized, finding positive reinforcement that works can be a challenging, but not impossible, task. Believe what you see, not what the students say.

4 Formulate and implement your reinforcement strategy.

Make key decisions and write a plan. After selecting the consequences that are most likely to work as positive reinforcement for your students, make the practical decisions necessary to implement an effective strategy. These suggestions should help you. After you read each guideline, briefly respond by filling in the corresponding space on Form 12.

1. Decide whom you are going to reinforce.

    Will it be the whole class, a small group, or one or two students?

Make sure you consider everyone whose behavior is important to the group dynamic. For example, you might include the student who uses disruptive, attention-seeking behavior, as well as the rest of the class, whom you encourage to ignore him/her.

2. Specify your target behavior(s).

    What specific behavior(s) are you going to consequate with positive reinforcement? If you have established any class rules (see Chapter 6), these decisions may already have been made.

    For special problems, short-term situations, and individual students with behavior problems, you might select one or two precise target behaviors.

    Make sure that your behaviors are specific and observable. A target like "improving self-esteem" is not useful; "making eye contact" or "volunteering answers" are great target behaviors.

3. Establish your criteria.

    Again, be as specific as possible. For example, criteria can be expressed as a percentage of total, a minimum number of responses, or a certain quality of responses. If you are vague about what you want and when you want it, it will be difficult to measure your progress toward your goals.

    Decide on an objective that is reasonable. Don't expect perfection! If you insist on 100%, every time, you are inviting disappointment for yourself and your students.

4. Decide what you will use for positive reinforcement.

    Review the surveys, questionnaires, menus, and other tools that you developed to identify student interests and preferences.

    Decide whether you want to use positive reinforcers from only one category (social reinforcers such as praise), or from a combination (compliments combined with a class-wide effort at earning a pizza party).

    Keep it inexpensive and easy. Use as many privileges, responsibilities, compliments, smiles, pats on the back, written comments, and other "free" reinforcers as possible.

5. Plan out your procedures.

    How often will you reinforce? For example, you may decide to deliver praise after each occurrence of the target behavior for newly learned skills, or intermittently for established, learned behaviors.

    Who will deliver reinforcement? If many people reinforce a behavior in many different settings and at various times, the behavior is more likely to increase quickly. It is also more likely to be maintained over time.

    Is your reinforcement system easy and practical? Strategies for behavior change should be efficient and simple. Time-consuming and complicated strategies will fail.

6. Establish a way to evaluate progress.

    Keep in mind that the older and the more established students are in their patterns of behavior, the longer it will take to change their old habits. Give your reinforcement plan a chance to work.

    Decide on a realistic time frame (often two to three weeks), and write down a date for evaluation of the program. When the date arrives, stop and evaluate.

Strive for objectivity. If possible, use a technique other than your own observation. Use a monitoring form to collect objective data (see Chapter 8), enlist an outside observer, invite student input, record behavior on videotape or audiotape, have students self-evaluate, and ask parents for input. Put all of your information together when you evaluate progress. This will help when you modify your plan.

7. Modify, revise, and adjust your plan.

    After evaluating the progress students are making, decide whether you want to continue the plan with changes, delete parts of it and add new ideas, or discontinue the plan. If you decide to discontinue because the goals have been met, you may want to continue intermittent reinforcement so that the behaviors are maintained at acceptable levels.

    In addition to evaluating students' progress, stop periodically to assess your overall system of positive reinforcement. If you think it's getting stale, change reinforcers and strategies, or introduce some novel techniques.

8. Decide how to reinforce yourself for a job well done.

    Teachers are sometimes perfectionists. They expect to be 100% effective,

100% of the time, with 100% of the students. Before you begin a new positive reinforcement plan, decide on how you will reward yourself for trying something new. A new pair of shoes, a dinner out with your best friend, a trip to the ice cream shop, or a Saturday alone might be just the boost you need. Appreciate your own hard work and your efforts to change.

Build enthusiasm and excitement.

When using positive reinforcement, take advantage of students' natural enthusiasm and interest. Use all of the tricks you know to make your class exciting, motivating, and interesting. Building suspense and anticipation by using raffles, games, and contests is important to overall classroom attitude. We have included sample reinforcement tools (Forms 13-15) that should make your system more interesting. Form 13, for example, shows raffle tickets which can be given to students as reinforcers. You can then hold a drawing for a prize. Some ideas for prizes include:

- Video game coupons
- Soft drinks
- Special pencils
- Baseball cards
- Fast food coupons
- Cassette tapes

5 Learn to use positive reinforcement in creative ways.

Try using it as a reductive technique. At the beginning of this chapter, we discussed the effect of positive reinforcement: an increase in the frequency of a target behavior. Several variations of positive reinforcement can also be used as reductive techniques to reduce undesirable behaviors without using punishment. Punishment decreases the frequency of a specific undesirable behavior; reductive positive reinforcement increases a desirable behavior. For example, reductive positive reinforcement can be used to:

- Reinforce a student for withholding a behavior (not hitting for ten minutes)

- Reinforce a student for a lower rate of behavior (whining fewer than five times in a 20-minute period)

- Reinforce a student for a behavior that is incompatible with the behavior that you want to reduce (sitting down instead of walking around)

In all of these scenarios, the goal is to reduce disruptive, annoying, or dangerous behavior by using positive reinforcement. This may be preferable for cases in which punishment is unlikely to be effective in the long term or in which you feel uncomfortable using punishment. Listed here are some practical suggestions for using reductive positive

Draw a square around a corner of the board, and write in the title, "Team Work; Team Win." Record positive behaviors by making tally marks in this space. The class works to earn a reward through individual participation and through group adherence to the rules.

When all students arrive on time to class, for example, put a tally mark in the class corner. To use peer pressure with a difficult student, tell the class, "If Barton brings his completed homework tomorrow, I will give this class three bonus points." Prearrange with the class that if they earn 50 points within one week, for instance, they will receive an ice cream treat or pizza party on Friday, or bonus points toward improving a grade.

Many teachers use class discussion to determine the kinds of rewards to establish. You can adapt the ideas to the particular classroom setting. Try to think of activities that enhance thinking and reading skills, but that students will still consider to be "rewards." For example, many students enjoy playing scholastic games, or reading the sports pages.

team work: team win

reinforcement in school. As with any reinforcement plan, you can always change your criteria, expecting better and better behavior from your students as the program continues. Try using positive reinforcement if:

- Johnny's tantrum lasts less than 20 minutes.

- Serena raises her hand instead of talking out.

- Betsy walks from the art room to English class without hitting anyone.

- Gene sits up instead of putting his head down on his desk.

- Anna curses fewer than two times during the class period.

- Ethan interrupts fewer than ten times today.

- Kat begins her math assignment without asking a question.

- Steve walks away instead of hitting when Hugo teases him.

- Francine makes it through an entire class period without complaining.

- Loren says "OK" instead of "I hate you."

- Billie smiles instead of glaring at you when she walks into the room.

- Wilton is fewer than ten minutes late to class.

Use it to improve group behavior. Peers are very influential, especially with adolescents and young adults. Developing a group contingency for positive reinforcement can be a quick , effective way to improve behavior. It is important, though, to focus on positive peer pressure. This means that students should encourage each other, not engage in blaming and criticism. In fact, it should be a requirement in your group plan that students engage only in positive reinforcement. There are many variations of group strategies for positive reinforcement. For example, a class could receive reinforcement

based on the behavior of one student (who is the "hero"), of a pair of good performers, of a small team that has improved, or for acceptable performance by everyone. Team

Work; Team Win (shown on the preceding page) is one strategy you might use for a group reinforcement plan.

Forms
for
Chapter

3

form 9 Rewards Menu (Elementary)

Name: _____

Ask each student to circle at least eight rewards that he/she would most like to earn in class.
(Read the list to non-readers, and help them mark the items they select.)

Duties

_____ Line leader
_____ Office messenger
_____ Class gardener
_____ Paper collector
_____ Pencil sharpener
_____ Eraser cleaner
_____ _____
_____ _____

Activities

_____ Computer time
_____ Quiet reading time
_____ Puzzle/game time
_____ Trip to the library
_____ Lunch with the teacher
_____ Time to draw or color
_____ _____
_____ _____

Other Goodies

_____ Ice cream
_____ Juice
_____ Soft drink
_____ Candy
_____ Fresh fruit
_____ _____
_____ _____

_____ Pencils
_____ Folders
_____ Extra notebook paper
_____ Art supplies
_____ Bookmarks
_____ Stickers
_____ _____
_____ _____

Group Rewards

_____ Extra recess time
_____ A five-minute "vacation" at the end of class
_____ A story read aloud by the teacher
_____ Popcorn and video party
_____ Listening to music

form 10 Rewards Menu (Secondary)

Name: _____ Class/Period:_____

Circle at least six items/activities you would like to earn in class.

Privileges/Responsibilities

_____ Messenger

_____ Supplies manager

_____ Music director
(chooses music to listen to)

_____ Photocopy maker

_____ Attendance checker

_____ Office assistant

_____ _____

_____ _____

Activities

_____ Computer time

_____ Trip to the library

_____ Lunch with the teacher

_____ Time to draw or color

_____ Having class outdoors

_____ Take a walk

_____ _____

_____ _____

Other Goodies

_____ Gum

_____ Ice cream

_____ Pretzels/chips

_____ Soft drink

_____ Candy

_____ Fresh fruit

_____ _____

_____ _____

_____ Blank cassette tapes

_____ Blank computer disks

_____ Pencils

_____ Folders

_____ Art supplies

_____ Post-it® notes

_____ _____

_____ _____

Group Rewards

_____ A five-minute "vacation" at
the end of class

_____ A story read aloud by
the teacher

_____ Bonus points on a grade

_____ Skipping a homework assignment

_____ Listening to music

form 11 What Works for You? (and, What Would You Work for?)

1. If you could spend time with anyone at school, who would it be? _____

2. If you had free time, what would you do? _____

   _____

   _____

3. If your teacher would let you go visit another room (or library, office, etc.) in the school, where would you go? _____

   _____

4. If you had a dollar (or two), what would you buy? _____

5. What is your favorite drink? _____

6. What is your favorite subject in school? _____

7. If you could earn time alone with the teacher, what would you like to do? _____

   _____

   _____

8. What is your favorite snack food? _____

9. If you could play any game you chose, what would it be? _____

   _____

10. Would you like it if good notes were sent home to your parent(s)? _____

form 12 Reinforcement Planning Form

1. Student or Class: _____

2. Target Behaviors: _____

   _____

   _____

3. Criteria: _____

   _____

   _____

   _____

   _____

4. What (Positive Reinforcers): _____

   _____

5. Procedures:

   How Often _____

   Person Who Will Reinforce_____

6. Evaluation:

   Information to be Reviewed_____ Target Date_____

7. Changes I Want to Make: _____

   _____

8. My Own Reward: _____

form 13 Raffle Tickets

Certificate for Outstanding Performance Awarded to: _____ 	Certificate for Outstanding Performance Awarded to: _____ 

Certificate for Outstanding Performance

Awarded to:

_____

Certificate for Outstanding Performance — Awarded to: (repeated across twelve tickets)

form 14 Amazing Turtles Leaping Hurdles

I, _____, agree to _____ during _____
time.

If I am successful, then I may color in a turtle. When all five of the turtles are colored in, I will get

_____.

Date: _____

Student:_____

Teacher: _____

Reprinted with permission from Jenson, W.R., Rhode, G, & Reavis, H.K. *The tough kid tool box.* Longmont, CO: Sopris West.

form 15 Take a Vacation

Take a Vacation
You have earned the privilege of skipping one homework assignment.

To redeem, fill in this information:

Class/Period: _____

Assignment: _____

Due Date: _____

Your Signature: _____

Teacher's Signature _____

*Turn in this coupon on the date the assignment would have been due.

Take a Vacation
You have earned the privilege of skipping one homework assignment.

To redeem, fill in this information:

Class/Period: _____

Assignment: _____

Due Date: _____

Your Signature: _____

Teacher's Signature _____

*Turn in this coupon on the date the assignment would have been due.

Take a Vacation
You have earned the privilege of skipping one homework assignment.

To redeem, fill in this information:

Class/Period: _____

Assignment: _____

Due Date: _____

Your Signature: _____

Teacher's Signature _____

*Turn in this coupon on the date the assignment would have been due.

Take a Vacation
You have earned the privilege of skipping one homework assignment.

To redeem, fill in this information:

Class/Period: _____

Assignment: _____

Due Date: _____

Your Signature: _____

Teacher's Signature _____

*Turn in this coupon on the date the assignment would have been due.

Take a Vacation
You have earned the privilege of skipping one homework assignment.

To redeem, fill in this information:

Class/Period: _____

Assignment: _____

Due Date: _____

Your Signature: _____

Teacher's Signature _____

*Turn in this coupon on the date the assignment would have been due.

Take a Vacation
You have earned the privilege of skipping one homework assignment.

To redeem, fill in this information:

Class/Period: _____

Assignment: _____

Due Date: _____

Your Signature: _____

Teacher's Signature _____

*Turn in this coupon on the date the assignment would have been due.

Take a Vacation
You have earned the privilege of skipping one homework assignment.

To redeem, fill in this information:

Class/Period: _____

Assignment: _____

Due Date: _____

Your Signature: _____

Teacher's Signature _____

*Turn in this coupon on the date the assignment would have been due.

Take a Vacation
You have earned the privilege of skipping one homework assignment.

To redeem, fill in this information:

Class/Period: _____

Assignment: _____

Due Date: _____

Your Signature: _____

Teacher's Signature _____

*Turn in this coupon on the date the assignment would have been due.

Take a Vacation
You have earned the privilege of skipping one homework assignment.

To redeem, fill in this information:

Class/Period: _____

Assignment: _____

Due Date: _____

Your Signature: _____

Teacher's Signature _____

*Turn in this coupon on the date the assignment would have been due.

encourage cooperation and compliance

The best way to deal with power struggles is to avoid them.

Ensuring that students do what is asked of them can be very difficult. Nevertheless, increasing students' cooperation and compliance with requests is a more positive strategy than engaging in "showdowns" with students. There are several ways that teachers can avoid unproductive and unpleasant power struggles.

Chapter 4

What to Do and How to Do it

1 Recognize the need to avoid power struggles whenever possible.

Know a power struggle when you see one. In school, teachers are faced with increasing numbers of students who do not recognize or appreciate a hierarchy of authority. They do not always believe that they should comply with the requests of the adults in the educational system. These same students may also challenge the authority of parents or community officials.

Students differ in the behaviors they use to avoid compliance and cooperation, in the degree of overt defiance they demonstrate, and in their willingness to escalate situations with authority figures. Their lack of cooperation varies on a continuum from passive uninvolvement to mild resistance to overt defiance, but the message is the same. When you find yourself in a situation with a student whose message is, "I'm not going to do it and you can't make me," you are caught in a power struggle.

Acknowledge that power struggles will occur. Students of any age, grade, gender, ability level, and background may resist teachers' requests. While we often think of older, larger students as the most resistant and difficult students to teach, even very young students today challenge teachers' authority. All teachers will face challenges to their authority at some point. Nevertheless, it is much more productive and pleasant to focus our energy on positive strategies for ensuring student cooperation than on making a reluctant student do something he/she doesn't want to do. The best way to deal with power struggles is to avoid them, which means taking steps to increase voluntary cooperation and compliance.

"Nothing is so strong as gentleness; nothing so gentle as real strength."

St. Francis de Sales

Accept the necessity for dealing quickly with noncompliance. Not every power struggle can be avoided. There are some students whose behavior is consistently oppositional and uncooperative; they are unlikely to change their habits and patterns of behavior. However, many other students are only occasionally noncompliant and resistant. It is often possible to increase their level of positive interaction and cooperation, and it is a good idea to take this type of proactive approach. Intervening in a pattern of escalating behavior before it becomes a full-fledged battle can prevent serious, demoralizing confrontations. You should respond positively and early to challenging behaviors, because if left unaddressed, noncompliance may:

- Diminish your authority

- Cause an emotional reaction in you and your students

- Have a "ripple effect"—make other students more difficult

- Keep the noncompliant student from learning what you want him/her to learn

- Cause the student to continue the "habit" of noncompliance

- Lead to a power struggle

2 Recognize that *everyone* is uncooperative sometimes.

Focus on why your students do not cooperate. Very few people do what is asked of them all of the time. Many of us will comply most of the time, but will occasionally resist or avoid tasks. It is important to recognize that students are just like adults. Sometimes they do what they are supposed to do, and sometimes they don't. Considering the various reasons for challenging and uncooperative behavior is the first step in changing the behavior. Once you know

---

Factor 1: The Person/People Making the Request

- Past relationships in the environment (school)
- History with this individual

Factor 2: The Nature of the Task

- Level of interest
- Level of enjoyment

Factor 3: Our Feelings of Competence

- Level of confidence in their ability
- Level of knowledge

Factor 4: The Timing of the Request

- How they're feeling (fatigue, health, drug/alcohol impairment or effects)
- Current level of stress/agitation
- Time of day

Factor 5: The Environmental Context

- The classroom climate

Factor 6: Their Satisfaction or Pleasure

- Their desire to assert power
- Enjoyment from watching a teacher or administrator become angry
- Enjoyment from being the center of attention

why students don't always do as they're asked

why the problem is occurring, you can tailor your approaches and responses to fit the individual situation. Begin by filling out the first two sections of Form 16. In these sections, you will describe the circumstances surrounding the student's noncompliance, in order to clarify what is happening and why. Then you should describe the student's actions, so that you can focus on improving specific, clearly identifiable behaviors.

3 Begin to work out solutions.

Explore a variety of possible approaches.
Students resist authority for many complicated reasons. There is no single strategy that will work for improving everyone's cooperation. You should consider many different options, then tailor each one to fit the student's age, response to positive reinforcement, level of cognitive functioning, and interpersonal strengths and weaknesses. One way to start is to use a brainstorming technique, such as the one we present in Chapter 7, to generate a list of interventions. Traditional responses often do not work with highly oppositional and challenging students; focus your energy on responding in ways that are new, innovative, and unusual. The ideas throughout this chapter will help get you started. It is also important that your list of possible interventions be as long as possible. Then, if one intervention does not work, you can try

- Increase student involvement by asking open-ended questions for which there are no right or wrong answers.
- Make sure that low-ability students are called on as often as high-achieving students are.
- Share your excitement about new ideas.
- Use assignments that require active involvement, such as independent studies and projects.
- Communicate your high expectations to your students.
- Use group assignments to increase motivation and also to teach cooperation skills.
- Invite parents, the principal, or others into your classroom. Audiences are great motivators.
- Check to see that your low-ability students have the needed academic survival skills. Do they need study skills instruction?
- Teach your students to persist when they encounter difficult situations.

strategies for motivating your students

something else. Think about what your goal is for this student's behavior. Record your goal and your chosen interventions in Sections 3 and 4 of Form 16.

Develop a specific plan of action.
Throughout this book, we emphasize the need for a systematic plan of action in response to everyday school problems. Because power struggles are so unpleasant, having a systematic plan for dealing with them is crucial. After you have examined the circumstances related to the student's noncompliance, identified the reason why he/she is uncooperative, specified your goal(s), and generated a list of possible responses, you can design your action plan.

Again, keep in mind that traditional approaches may not be effective, so you may need to try something unique or unusual. Use Section 5 of the planning form to help you articulate your ideas. Try to be very clear about your evaluation criteria and allow enough time for change to take place (start with two weeks).

4 Change your instructional style.

Make your instruction more motivating.
The topic of motivation will be addressed more thoroughly in Chapter 14. However, whenever student cooperation

- Give students checklists of steps or directions and let them check off each completed item.
- Save completed projects and papers to use as samples, examples, and models.
- Teach your students rhymes, chants, mnemonics, and other memory devices.
- Highlight key words on tests and worksheets; make sure students understand the directions.
- Give students slot outlines and let them fill in the blanks during direct instruction.
- Let non-disabled students be "peer note takers" for those who have attention, motor, visual, or eye-hand coordination problems. Note takers can use carbon paper, or their notes can be photocopied to give to others.
- Allow students to be study partners.
- Use games and contests whenever you need to drill and practice.
- Teach your students visual imagery techniques.
- Let students use tools like tape recorders, calculators, etc. when it fits the lessons.
- Encourage parents, grandparents, and volunteers to come into your classroom for conversation and sharing.
- Use the media to grab students' interest.
- Extend students' learning with special events that parents and others can join.

add variety to your instruction

and compliance is an issue, motivation is an important consideration. While a motivating instructional environment cannot guarantee student interest and involvement, it will prevent some of the problems that arise when students feel that their schoolwork is boring or irrelevant. Throughout this section of the chapter, you will find suggestions to begin to improve motivation in your classroom.

Add variety to your instruction. If adults had to sit through six or seven hours of school day after day, many of us would be bored and restless. It is the same with students. When a teacher's instruction is repetitive and dull or when a teacher merely talks to students instead of involving them in the learning process, student interest and excitement wanes. One easy way to combat this is to vary your instructional style. You can

increase variety in your classroom with the simple techniques on this page.

Use fun reading materials. Many students have difficulty in school because they can't read. More than any other academic skill, reading is essential for school success because we use reading skills in everything we do at school. When students are bored by reading, find materials that are different, interesting, and fun. Use these materials in your instruction by integrating them into thematic chapters, supplementing the regular text material with them, and using them as a basis for group activities. Interesting reading materials may get reluctant learners involved and decrease their resistance and noncompliance. Try these:

- Classified ads from the newspaper
- Travel magazines
- Joke books
- Catalogues
- Driver's Education manuals
- The sports section of the newspaper
- Cookbooks
- Greeting cards
- Cover jackets from tapes and CDs (after your scrutiny and approval)
- Comic strips
- Advice columns from magazines and newspapers
- Television listings and schedules

- Airline or bus schedules
- Advertisements
- Telephone books, especially the yellow pages

Adapt students' written assignments.

Written reports are a useful culmination of research experience, but they can become routine when used too often or to the exclusion of other products. Students who are less competent at writing than they would like to be are often resistant when presented with a written assignment. They may procrastinate, stall, and fail to begin their projects. Listed here are some suggestions for modifying or replacing written reports. These options are highly motivating for those students who are unlikely to complete more traditional papers. When students can produce written work in a format they enjoy, they are more likely to cooperate.

5 Use precorrections and clear requests.

"Set students up" for success. When you anticipate that a student will be unlikely to cooperate, it sometimes helps if you provide the student with guidance before he/she is expected to comply. Remind the student of what you expect, provide a cue or warning of the time limit you have in mind, and explain how you expect the student to carry out your instructions. For example, when a

student must end a highly-preferred activity (like using the computer) and begin one that is not as desirable (like a written assignment), you might say, "Sonia, in two minutes, computer time will be over. When your time is up, I'm going to ask you to turn off the computer and get out your English book, some paper, and a pen. I want you to say 'OK,' turn off the computer, and move to your desk. You have two more minutes."

When you can't persuade a teenager to do what you want, you may also appeal to his/her oppositional nature:

- "You know, I would ask you to help me with this but I know you're not interested."
- "This isn't something we can do. I think we need an expert."
- "I'll bet you can't finish these assignments in ten minutes."

Let Them Do it Their Way!

- Selling a book idea or concept—students convince the rest of the class that their idea or product is best
- Radio broadcasts—students act as news reporters broadcasting descriptions of exciting events
- Illustrations—students illustrate a sequence of events or experiments
- Letters—students write letters to authors, athletes, politicians, educators, and community leaders on important topics
- Models—students build models of buildings, molecules, inventions, etc.
- Cartoons—students draw panel cartoons illustrating some humorous part of a story or event
- Diaries and journals—students write diaries as if they were a character in a text or were a famous author
- Visual timelines—students develop visual timelines of historical events or biographical information
- Displays—students depict sequences of events with murals, detailing historical occurrences or scientific progressions
- Dramatizations, plays, scenarios—students write short plays incorporating the action of their report or dramatizing an exciting event from their reading

report options

Adapted with permission from Murphy, D.A., Meyers, C.C., Olesen, S., McKean, K., Custer, S.H. (1995). *Exceptions: A handbook of inclusion activities for teachers of students at grades 6-12 with mild disabilities.* Longmont, CO: Sopris West. All rights reserved.

Use an effective sequence to make your requests. When making requests or giving directions to noncompliant or uncooperative students, the way you make the request may be just as important as what you are asking. Try a sequence of instructions that is clear and firm, yet allows students to keep their dignity. A modified precision request sequence is one way to approach your resistant students and increase the chances that they will comply with your requests. The basics of this format are presented here:

- Give one direction at a time.

- Don't ask. Say "Please . . ." If you ask, you may give students a chance to say "no."

- Be close enough for the student to hear you, but not close enough to be intrusive (about three feet away).

- Use a firm but soft tone of voice. If you challenge loudly in front of the whole class, the student may feel the need to resist in order to save face in front of peers.

- Move away and give the student time to comply. Reinforce him/her for complying.

- If the student doesn't do what you asked, restate the direction, using stronger phrasing (e.g., "You need to . . .").

- Don't be sarcastic.

- Don't give ultimatums.

- Try to give directions that ask students to start something. Sometimes, it's easier to get them to start something than to stop something.

- Try not to talk too much. Give only important directions.

- Be clear about what will happen if a student does not do what you ask.

Adapted with permission from Rhode, G., Jenson, W.R., and Reavis, H.K. (1993). *The tough kid book: Practical classroom management strategies.* Longmont, CO: Sopris West. All rights reserved.

6 Change your students' habits.

Teach them a new response. Sometimes students get into a habit of saying "no" and will automatically refuse a request even before they know what it is. When students are so habitually noncompliant that their first reaction is to resist or refuse to cooperate, it may be necessary to change their habitual pattern of behavior. One way to do this is to teach a new response that is acceptable, then reinforce them for using it. One version of this strategy is the OK Game. Print or copy a supply of coupons or tickets with "OK" on them (a master page is provided on Form 17). Use the tickets in one or more of these ways: First, each student can be given a specified number of tickets, which are labeled with his/her name. Each time the student says "OK" when given a direction, he/she puts one ticket in a raffle jar. You can then hold periodic drawings for reinforcers. Second, you can use the tickets as immediate reinforcers, presenting a student with one each time he/she says, "OK." Or, finally, you can use the tickets in a group game, in which the class is rewarded if everyone says "OK" at least two times during the day. There are many other ways to use the OK coupons; however, it is important to remember to teach students how and when to respond, and to use positive reinforcement whenever they say "OK" instead of something less agreeable.

T eachers are always told to be specific about the way they praise students' appropriate and desirable behavior. So, when you want to increase cooperation, catch them cooperating, then praise them for it. Say "Thanks for cooperating," or "Thanks for doing what I asked," not "Thanks for sitting still," or "Thanks for raising your hand." *Praise students for the act of cooperating, not just for the tasks they perform.*

catch them cooperating

Encourage a chain of cooperative behaviors. One way to increase the likelihood that habitually noncompliant students will cooperate is to establish positive behavioral momentum. This can be done by chaining together a sequence of cooperative behaviors. Make a series of high-probability requests (things the student likes to do or is going to do anyway). Then make your low-probability request (the thing the student really doesn't want to do). Reinforce the student for following each of your directions. Here is an example:

- First, give some directions that you know the student is likely to follow.

    - "Come on in the room. Thanks!"
    - "Hang up your coat. All right."
    - "Have a seat. Good job!"
    - "Take a minute and relax. That's good."
    - "Here, have a sheet of paper. We're right on track."

- Then, in a matter-of-fact-way, make the request that is likely to be refused.

    - "Take out your math book and open it to page 27."

- Make sure you reinforce the student for complying.

    - "Thanks for following my directions. Good work."

7 Hold students accountable.

Use some tools to help you. Ultimately, it is the student's choice to cooperate or not. When a student digs in his/her heels and decides he/she is not going to work, there may not be a lot you can do about it at the moment. Rather than becoming involved in an escalating power struggle that could eventually require physical intervention, you may decide to reconsider your options and design a new plan. However, it is important to encourage the student to take responsibility for his/her decision. Form 18 is one way to encourage student accountability. This form documents a student's lack of cooperation and will provide you with useful information. If the student refuses to sign the form, fill in the information anyway and note that the student refused to sign. It is important to record this extreme level of noncompliance.

Have students self-record and self-monitor. Chapter 15 provides some practical information to help you increase students' skills in monitoring and controlling their own behavior. It is impossible to make students do things they refuse to do. Engaging in unproductive and stressful battles of control with them leaves everyone upset. These power struggles also interfere with instruction. If you have tried all of the strategies in this chapter and you still find yourself locked in conflict with resistant students, consider focusing your energy on teaching your students to self-monitor, self-manage, and deal with the consequences if they don't. Here are some final thoughts on avoiding power struggles:

- Be clear about your consequences.

- Look students in the eye when asking them to do something. Be direct.

- Use humor when you can. It may defuse the situation.

- Use reverse psychology: "Whatever you do, please don't . . ."

- Assume a non-threatening body posture and a relaxed tone of voice, but be ready to follow through.

- Try a friendly dare: "I'll bet you can't . . . in five minutes."

- Appeal to your students' maturity and experience: "I know that you are too bright and too mature to make a poor choice. I'm confident that you will be smart about this and choose to . . ."

- Give students time to think about their actions.

- Let a student save face in front of peers. Move the conversation out to the hall if possible.

- Don't argue.

Forms
for
Chapter

4

form 16 How I'm Going to Encourage _____ to Do What I Ask

1. **The Circumstances:** _____'s noncompliance and lack of cooperation occurs:

   When: _____

   With Whom: _____

   In What Class: _____

   This is why I think the noncompliance occurs: _____

   _____

2. **The Behavior:** Right now, _____ demonstrates his/her noncompliance by: _____

   _____

   This is how often he/she does it: _____

   He/she escalates to defiance and/or threats of aggression if: _____

3. **My goal** is for the student to: _____

4. **Interventions I Could Try:** _____

   _____

   These are the people who can help me: _____

5. **My Action Plan:** I will begin to intervene when _____ does this: _____

   My first intervention will be to: _____

   If that doesn't work, I will: _____

   I'm going to try this plan for _____ weeks/days and evaluate on: _____

   This is how I will know if my plan is working: _____

form 17

form 18 Refusal to Work

When a student is passively refusing to work, approach the student with a statement along these lines: "I am not going to harass you into doing your work, but if you are going to choose not to work, I want you to sign this statement."

You may want to implement a consequence after a certain number of forms have been signed (a letter or phone call to the parent, for example). Students may be reluctant to document the fact that they are choosing not to work; if a student has not signed the form after five to eight minutes, quietly pick the form up, take it back to your desk, and make a note on the form that the student refused to sign it. Also note the current date.

Student:_____ Date:_____ Period:_____

Class: _____ Teacher:_____

I made the decision not to work in class today because:

_____ 1. I did not bring the proper materials to class (pen, paper, textbook, etc.).

_____ 2. I did not understand/was not interested in the assignment.

_____ 3. I fell asleep.

_____ 4. I was tired/bored/unable to concentrate.

_____ 5. I wanted to assert my independence.

_____ 6. Other:

I understand that my choice not to work in class will result in a zero (0) for my daily grade. I also understand that when I make a zero, I am seriously hurting my chances of passing the course.

Student's Signature: _____

teach positive social skills

Social skills can be learned. Positive social skills will improve students' chances for success in school, work, and interpersonal relationships.

While demonstrating good social skills has always been important, social skills instruction has not always been a component of school curricula. However, increasing numbers of students are coming to school without having mastered even the most basic competencies required for good interpersonal relationships, effective cooperation in a group, or self-management in stressful and demanding situations. Teaching social skills can have a positive impact on everyone.

Chapter 5

What to Do and How to Do it

1 Develop a positive attitude toward social skills instruction.

Consider why you should teach social skills. There are many reasons why teachers are reluctant to teach social skills. They include:

- "Parents should teach social skills at home. It's not my job."

- "I'm not a special education teacher. I don't know anything about teaching social skills."

- "Students already know how to behave. They just don't do it because they're 'bad,' 'lazy,' or 'stubborn.'"

These arguments are not necessarily invalid. Parents probably should be teaching social skills; teachers don't always get the training they need in how to teach social skills; and some students do, in fact, know

how to behave appropriately but choose not to do so. Despite these concerns, it may be in everyone's best interest if students were provided with social skills instruction in school. Moreover, since students with disabilities and/or behavior problems are, more often than ever before, included in regular education classes, there is no such thing as "just teaching regular education" anymore. Finally, there are some students who will learn social skills only if they are provided with direct, systematic instruction;

numerous opportunities to practice their skills; and consistent, effective positive reinforcement to make it worth their while to use the skills.

Be clear about what social skills are. Social skills instruction is not counseling. If you are going to teach social skills as part of a comprehensive curriculum, it is a good idea to define your goals by first defining what you mean by social skills. Social skills can be defined in many ways; these three definitions address relevant aspects of social skills, and may be useful as starting points to begin your planning. We can think of social skills as:

● The abilities we need for effective interpersonal functioning

● The behaviors (both verbal and non-verbal) we use to influence our environment

● Our ability to relate to others and to modify our behavior as the environment requires

It is the third definition that we believe is the most important, because it implies the need for flexible responses that change with the demands of various situations. These are the skills that so many students seem to lack. Their responses are not flexible; they speak, act, and respond the same way regardless of the people, circumstances, or requirements of the situation. The high level of

social awareness and behavioral self-control required to develop flexible responses is difficult for teachers to teach but critical for students to learn.

"With all beings and all things we shall be as relatives."   Sioux Nation

---

2 Focus on the skills that students need.

Familiarize yourself with age-appropriate skills. One way to begin your selection of which social skills to teach is to look at some lists of social skills from published curricula. The table of contents from a commercial social skills program can provide

suggestions for skills you may not have thought of, but which your students need. Here is a list of skills to get you started; you can find additional information in *Social Skills in the School* (Black, Downs, Bastien, Brown, & Wells, 1987) and *Skillstreaming the Elementary School Child* (McGinnis & Goldstein, 1984). Both are good sources for target skills.

Diagnose your students. First, try to determine the skills your students need to learn. You can use one or more of these strategies to identify the social skills most needed by your students:

● Rely on observation:

– Watch your students in action to see which skills they lack.

Relating to Others
 • Building friendships
 • Maintaining friendships
 • Apologizing
 • Compromising/negotiating
 • Giving/accepting praise or criticism

Personal Responsibility
 • Goal setting
 • Decision making
 • Assuming responsibility
 • Promptness
 • Asking for assistance

Coping With Stress
 • Handling frustration
 • Coping with anger
 • Dealing with stress
 • Accepting others' authority
 • Resisting peer pressure

Personal/Affective Development
 • Building self-esteem
 • Coping with depression
 • Coping with anxiety
 • Controlling impulsivity
 • Sensitivity to others

target social skills

Reprinted with permission from McCarron, L.T., Fad, K.M., & McCarron, M.B. (1992). *Achieving behavioral competencies: A program for developing social/emotional skills with secondary students.* Dallas, TX: McCarron-Dial Systems.

- Have someone else observe and give you feedback.

- Use commercial social skills instruments (available in many publishers' catalogs):

    - Use a quick, simple rating scale.
    - Have parents or other caregivers rate the students.

- Ask your students:

    - Find out which skills they think would improve the class.
    - Ask them what skill deficits bother them the most.

- Identify the skills they need most:

    - Use your research to help you determine the highest-priority skills.
    - Ask other teachers what's most important to them.

- Use their Individualized Education Programs (IEPs):

    - For students in special education, make sure you follow their written IEPs.
    - Especially for students with emotional/behavioral problems, write some social skills goals into the IEPs.

3 Determine the nature of students' skill deficits.

Don't make assumptions. Social skills and behavior management are closely entwined. Often, it is difficult to know when a student has failed to master some critical social skill, when he/she has a serious emotional or neurological disorder, or when there are other environmental variables complicating the issue. Before you make assumptions about motives, desires, or reasons, take the time to accumulate relevant information. Observe the student, talk to his/her parent(s) and former teachers, read the student's records, and ask the student for information about how and why he/she behaves. Then, if you need more help from a consultant or behavior specialist, ask for it before you begin your social skills teaching program.

Look for the reasons behind poor skill use. Students may fail to demonstrate a specific social skill for several different reasons. First, they may not have been taught the skill. For example, many children grow up and go through school without being taught how to compromise or negotiate, so they may not compromise when they're working on a group project. Second, some students have been taught a skill but don't use it. For example, many students have been taught good listening skills since they were in kindergarten. However, they often fail to use their listening skills, because they enjoy talking to their friends more than listening to the teacher. Finally, some students have been taught a social skill and can use it under normal circumstances, but fail to maintain enough self-control when they're stressed or overexcited to demonstrate the

PUTTING IT TOGETHER

PART ONE **5** teach positive social skills

form 19 What We Want to See/What We Want to Hear

The skill _____ *Coping With Anger* _____

(target skill)

should look and sound like this in our classroom (or school):

What We Want to See (specific behaviors)	What We Want to Hear (specific behaviors)
1. Hands by your sides	1. "I"-statements
2. Arm length away from the other person	2. Quiet voice, no yelling
3. Neutral facial expression, no glaring or scowling	3. Respectful language, no cursing

skill. Before you automatically assume that you need to teach every social skill possible, evaluate your students' proficiencies to determine whether the issue is teaching, reinforcement, or self-control.

4 Plan an instructional sequence.

Clearly define the skills you're going to teach. One good way you can define what specific behaviors you value is to use a T-chart like the one on Form 19. Use it to break down each of your target social skills

into its components. (A sample is provided here of a completed T-chart.) This chart will help students by clearly defining the specific behaviors required for each social skill. The chart should also make your teaching easier, because you know exactly which behaviors to focus on during instruction.

Decide on a logical, effective teaching strategy. When teachers plan academic instruction, they usually follow a commonly accepted sequence that has been validated by research and practice. Usually, the instructional design includes introductory activities, review of prior learning, direct

instruction, guided and independent practice, and extension (generalization) activities. In social skills instruction, it is especially important to focus on generalization of skills, because many students who have had social skills instruction still fail to demonstrate their skills in other settings and with other individuals. A typical instructional sequence for social skills might be as follows:

- Determine which skills students need and which they have already mastered.

- Prioritize the skills you want to teach. Decide on a logical order in which to teach them (usually a hierarchy).

- Decide on specific objectives.

- Gather relevant curricular materials. Make sure lessons are age-appropriate and are motivating to students.

- Then, focus on how you will teach the skills, including:

  - Guiding students' self-awareness so that they learn to recognize their feelings and reactions in particular situations
  - Teacher instruction
  - Teacher demonstration (modeling)
  - Student interaction (role play)
  - Self-management and generalization strategies

- Supplement your direct instruction with a variety of additional techniques, including:

  - Prompting and coaching
  - Strategic placement (putting students in situations with good, natural role models)
  - Relevant literature
  - Taped materials (audio and video)
  - Peer mediation training
  - Cooperative learning groups

- Make plans to include parents and school personnel in the teaching process.

5 Set up social skills learning groups.

Make some basic decisions about group structure. Social skills are best taught in groups. This is a natural approach, since social skills are essential in almost every group interaction. (You can find detailed information on group learning structures in Chapter 13.) When setting up social skills groups in your classroom, first designate one or two students to be group leaders. If possible, find another adult to help you to model and role play, and to manage the group during instruction. Instructional assistants, parents, or volunteers would be best; however, older students can also be excellent models for your class. Once you've structured your groups, then decide on a rotating schedule, so that everyone

has a chance to try each role. Most social skills curricula provide excellent suggestions for modeling and role play scenarios, including sample dilemmas and situations that require positive social skills.

Set the group rules. Anytime students are interacting in groups, there should be guidelines about what is acceptable and what is not. This is especially true when adults and students model skills and when students role play, because if students are not courteous and polite, it may be impossible for the modeling and role play to be effective. Keep the group rules simple, but clear, such as:

- Only person at a time can speak.

- Feedback must always include a positive comment or suggestion.

- No attacks or put-downs.

6 Make your instruction work.

Follow some key guidelines. Instruction in social skills can be structured the same way as academic lessons, using direct instruction, modeling, and student practice to help students master new skills. Students who truly do not know the appropriate words or actions in interpersonal situations must receive direct instruction. Because social skills require demonstrated, observable behaviors, this direct instruction is often in the form of adult modeling. And just as with new academic skills, mastery of new social skills will require practice in class and at home, sometimes by student role play. If your modeling and role play are to be effective, you should follow some of these procedures:

- Use a variety of friendly models who reflect the students' ages and socioeconomic status, and who represent both genders.

- Be clear and detailed in your actions.

Students love to play games. Make classroom games a time to practice social skills. Put students in groups and allow them to choose a favorite board game. While they play, monitor them on specific social skills like complimenting others, encouraging others, taking turns, and being a good winner or loser.

group games

- Progress from least to most difficult skills.

- Use several different models.

- Teach in as many natural settings as possible (lunchroom, library, hallway, bus, etc.).

- Show steps in the correct order.

- Plan and practice scenarios and role play before you use them with your class.

- Use lots of positive reinforcement for students after their role play.

- Reward improvement.

- Give lots of practice, including homework.

Keep things interesting. If all you do in social skills instruction is modeling and role play every day, you and your students will

lose interest quickly. Good teachers use a variety of techniques during their instruction. Packaged curricula, sequential programmed instruction, videotapes, audiotapes, games, posters, computer software, books, workbooks, and many other resources have been developed in recent years for social skills instruction. (Examples are provided on Forms 20 and 21.) Familiarize yourself with as many of these resources as you can, choose a variety of materials, and design your lessons using several different approaches. Use cooperative activities, games, and natural opportunities to teach social skills all day long. Take the time to plan your chapters and lessons, just as you plan academic instruction. In the resource list, you will find information about related materials that are helpful for teachers and administrators who are interested in beginning classroom or school-wide social skills programs.

Make the most of natural opportunities. Everyone in school uses social skills all day long in many different situations. Chapter 13 offers suggestions for building students' social skills during cooperative activities. You should also be on the lookout for natural, incidental situations in which you can emphasize students' use of social skills. The unstructured situations in which students may have the most difficulty doing well socially are some of the best opportunities to teach by modeling, reminders, and coaching.

Focus on places where students are most likely to interact, including:

- In the cafeteria
- On the playground
- In special subjects and fine arts classes
- At special school events
- On the bus
- In the hallways
- In the library, computer room, and laboratories

Model respect for others in your classroom. When you speak to teachers, students, parents, and other staff, demonstrate your own good manners. Be polite and considerate, don't interrupt, and most of all, don't gossip.

7 Monitor and reinforce.

Keep up with monitoring. In Chapter 8, we discuss monitoring of behavior. Form 40 in that chapter may be helpful in checking on students' use of social skills. Simply fill in the target social skills in the spaces provided. Form 31 in Chapter 6 can also be helpful; it is a group monitoring form which is great for recording anecdotal observations. These forms can be adapted and modified to fit your situation and your own teaching style, and are useful reminders of the need to monitor and evaluate social as well as academic skills.

Make it worth their while to use social skills. If no one notices or responds to students who are using positive social skills, students are unlikely to continue to use the skills. We have already discussed positive reinforcement in some detail, so it isn't necessary to discuss all of the principles again here. However, it is important that students who are learning to use good social skills be consistently reinforced with significant, powerful reinforcers. Pay special attention to reinforcing improvement, not just mastery. For those students who have few social

To encourage students to practice good social behavior on the bus, give each student a small "report card" that can be quickly and easily stamped by the bus driver. Students get a stamp for good behavior each morning and afternoon, then they can earn goodies for their stamps on Fridays.

stamp collecting

skills, or very poor ones, make sure you provide lots of reinforcement as they begin to learn and use their new skills.

Forms
for
Chapter
5

form 19 What We Want to See/What We Want to Hear

The skill_____

(target skill)

should look and sound like this in our classroom (or school):

What We Want to See (specific behaviors)	What We Want to Hear (specific behaviors)
1.	1.
2.	2.
3.	3.
4.	4.

form 20 Anger Express

Step 1

Stop and Calm Down

"I won't blow up."

Step 2

Think

"What will happen if I lose my temper?"

Step 3

Talk

"I'm mad about . . . ." "I want . . . ."

Step 4

Feel Good Again

Forgive and Forget

1. Read the words in the circles.
2. Cut out the circles.
3. Match the circles to the wheels.
4. Paste on the circles.
5. Color.

ANGER EXPRESS

Stop   Think   Talk   Feel Good Again

form 2 1 "Calm-Down" Thoughts

Think about why these people might be frustrated, then suggest some things they can say to themselves to keep from getting upset.

PART TWO

Planning for Positive Behavior

define your expectations and establish clear rules

Every group must have expectations and rules in order to function successfully.

School rules are usually designed to regulate behavior so that teachers can teach and students can learn. In the classroom, teachers can encourage desirable, positive student behaviors through high expectations and clearly-defined limits. The designing, teaching, and implementing of rules and guidelines are essential components of effective preventive discipline.

Chapter 6

What to Do and How to Do it

1 Teach your students about rules and consequences.

Teach definitions of the terms. Rules define the behaviors that are expected and acceptable in a classroom, and they delineate behaviors that are unacceptable and prohibited. Consequences, on the other hand, occur as a result of something. Consequences are contingent; that is, they only occur if something else happens first. They can also be either positive or negative. For example, rewards and praise are positive consequences; punishments, withholding privileges, and scolding are negative consequences. To be most effective, consequences must always be provided immediately after they are earned.

Explain the difference between the terms. Rules and consequences do not have to be part of the same statement. We can state a rule without stating the specific consequence for disobeying the rule. In our society, rules are often stated separately from their consequences. For example, a "No Left Turn" sign states the rule about turning, but it does not tell you what the consequence will be if you disobey this rule. Also, a specific consequence does not always have to be paired with a specific rule. Different consequences can be applied when you break a particular rule, depending on how many times you have violated the rule, how severe the violation is, and other circumstances. (While this chapter is focused on rules, the following chapter will discuss effective selection and implementation of consequences.)

Conduct discussions. A classroom discussion on rules and consequences is important in order to explain these two terms. Modify your discussion to fit your students' ages and levels of understanding, and ask questions to check their comprehension. Making sure that rules are understood has important implications for teacher and administrator responses. If a student is unaware of a rule and does something that breaks the rule, our response would probably be to teach the student what the rule is and why it is used, and to give examples of behaviors that comply and do not comply with the rule. However, if the student is aware of the rule and then does something to disobey it, we can assume that he/she made a conscious choice to disobey the rule. We would probably then use consequences designed to reinforce rule compliance or to punish rule-breaking behavior.

2 Decide on appropriate rules for your classroom.

Consider your students. When deciding on the rules for your classroom, make your choices fit your group. Even though teachers may work with the same grade level or subject for several years, the population of students changes. Individual classes have unique group characteristics, including interaction styles, leadership issues, problems, strengths, and interpersonal dynamics. Some rules will be necessary and appropriate for one group but not for another. Work with your students to decide on rules that meet your needs. Define each rule for your students. Examples are provided here to get you started:

- Do not hurt yourself or others—Keep your hands and feet to yourself; avoid fights.

- Do not say mean things—No put-downs; use positive comments whenever you can.

- Think before you do something—Calm yourself before you react; think before you speak.

- Do not bother others—Don't interrupt others or keep them from learning.

- Be a good friend—Say and do things that will make others feel good about themselves; use praise and compliments.

- Respect others—Respect others' space and property; don't steal or cheat.

- Be where you are supposed to be—Be in your seat when you're supposed to be; listen to directions.

- Be an independent learner—Do what you should do without being told.

Explain the rationale for each rule. The rationale for each rule should be understandable and acceptable to students, and should be open for discussion. You should never use the phrase "Because I said so!" as the rationale for a rule. If you cannot explain why you have the rule, you probably do not need it. State rules in language that students will understand. For all students, but especially those who are very young, it is wise to write your rules in a short version. You can still discuss the rules in a thorough and complete manner, but short, simple rules are easier for students to learn and remember.

3 Make sure everyone clearly understands the rules.

Give positive and negative examples of each rule. When teaching most concepts, teachers use positive examples to illustrate the concept and to provide students with a framework for understanding similarities. Teachers also use negative examples, or non-examples, to help students understand differences. Rules can be taught in much the same way. You can and should provide both positive and negative examples of each rule, giving students opportunities to ask questions, clarify information, and present hypothetical situations for review.

Teach lessons on specific rules. Form 22 shows an example of how you might structure a lesson on rules. Use this format as a teaching guide for your classroom rules, and develop a lesson on each rule. In this example, the rule is stated in a short form, the rationale for the rule is given, the rule is defined, and some negative and positive examples of behaviors are provided. Please note that the behaviors presented are examples designed to illustrate possible choices. For younger students, those with limited cognitive skills, or those with learning style variations, select examples appropriate for the particular classroom or situation. Teachers in regular education classes or those who teach very young children may wish to teach only a few rules. Teachers in very restrictive environments for students with serious emotional/behavioral disorders may wish to structure many lessons on rules.

Post the rules and consequences in your classroom. All rules and negative consequences (punishments) that will be used in your classroom should be explained in advance. They should also be posted in full view of all the students, so that the rules are stated directly and clearly. It is unfair, unethical, and unwise to apply negative consequences for rule infractions without informing the students ahead of time. Doing so causes students to feel betrayed, angry, resentful, and distrustful. If negative consequences are applied in this way very often, you can expect rebellion against the consequences. The rules should be defined clearly enough for students to know exactly what they are and to understand what is allowed or not allowed. Forms 23-25 are sample rule posters that combine rule messages with attractive artwork.

❹ Check your students' understanding of the rules.

After initial teaching, evaluate. After we teach a new academic skill or introduce a new concept, we usually check students' understanding and mastery of the content. We should do the same with classroom rules. There are several ways that this can be done. First, you can use oral questioning techniques. Simple questions to determine if students understand what the rules are and what they mean can be very effective. You may also wish to give a written test. For very young students, symbols like smiley faces can be used to indicate understanding. Older students can provide written answers to questions and can check off correct responses on check sheets. Sample tests are presented at the end of the chapter. Form 26 is appropriate for younger students; Form 27 can be used with older students. You should also have periodic reviews of the rules (once per day, once per week, or whenever needed) and positively reinforce students who demonstrate their understanding.

Use peer evaluations. You can also have peers check each other for understanding and mastery with a simple "Turn to Your Partner" technique. Directions like "Turn to your partner and tell him/her what our rule is about hitting," or "Turn to your partner and give him/her an example of how to get along with others," are effective with students of almost any age.

5 Help students relate rules to their everyday lives.

Give them plenty of practice. Students who are learning the class rules should be provided with both guided and independent practice on the rules. In class, you can use role play, modeling, and corrective feedback. You can also provide opportunities and reinforcement for practicing the rule behaviors at home. Homework assignments are an excellent way of involving parents in the process, so that they know the rules, too. Forms and worksheets can simplify the process of monitoring and reinforcing rule behaviors. Form 28 is a contract for use by teachers; Form 29 is a more open-ended homework form for parents to use with their children.

Pay attention to normal, everyday procedures. Most of us will have to follow rules and procedures throughout our lives. Some of the rules will be explicit, and some will be implicit. We must learn to respect and follow both types of rules. It is just as important for students to follow the routines that occur regularly and naturally in school as it is for them to comply with formally posted rules. When they fail to follow the expected everyday procedures, their behavior may become disruptive to other students' learning and to your teaching. On this page is a quick and easy checklist that you can

Do all of your students know your rules and procedures about:

- Attendance/tardies
- Beginning-of-period activities
- Out-of-room policies
- Materials/what to bring to class
- Pencil sharpener use
- Student access to teacher's desk, storage, other materials
- End-of-period routines
- Student attention/participation
- Seatwork policies:
  - Talking
  - Asking for help

- Out-of-seat
- What to do when finished
- Group work:
  - Assigning students to groups
  - Use of materials and supplies
- Behavior during interruptions
- Make-up work
- Extra help/tutoring
- Lockers
- Bathroom and drinking fountain use

how do you manage these rules and procedures?

use to assess everyone's level of knowledge about the day-to-day routines in your room.

Check your classroom arrangement. One factor that is often overlooked in a classroom is its floor plan. Remember, everything in the room impacts everything else. A well-designed classroom can actually improve the likelihood that students will follow the rules and procedures, since it will be easy and convenient to do so.

Think about your students and your classroom routines, and structure the classroom arrangement to facilitate your procedures and accommodate your particular students. For example, now that so many students with special needs are included in general

education classrooms, you should organize your furniture and materials so that lecture, large-group, and small-group instruction can all be accommodated with a minimum of disruption. Also, be sure that critical sections like listening and learning centers and reading areas are provided. Finally, be sure that you consider student seating arrangements, in case pencil sharpeners, bathrooms, water fountains, and high-traffic areas become a problem or a temptation for some students.

Form 30 presents a sample floor plan for a classroom. When arranging your classroom, consider several variables, including traffic patterns, lighting, adequate space, seating arrangements, accessibility of supplies, etc. Here are some good questions that we asked ourselves when we designed the plan shown on the form:

- Can students enter and leave the room without disturbing those in the quiet areas of the room?

- Are there separate areas for large and small group instruction, so that one group does not distract the others?

- Is there ample space for everyone, so that students don't feel as if they're "on top of each other"?

- Does the group instruction area include blackboards that are close enough for students to read easily from their seats?

- Can students easily reach the supplies they need?

- Is the teacher's desk close to the door for easy access in an emergency?

- Is there space set aside for those students who need a quiet area in which to work?

- Have you considered the lighting in arranging the furniture? Will students have enough light at their work areas to perform their tasks?

- Does the room look clean, organized, and uncluttered? Is it free of distractions?

6 Constantly monitor students' performance.

Evaluate how well students know and follow the rules. Designing, teaching, practicing, and evaluating students' performance on classroom rule behaviors is critical for preventing behavior problems. Waiting until the rules have been broken means that instead of teaching, you must spend your time responding to a negative or undesirable behavior. There are many ways for teachers to monitor students, or to teach students to evaluate for themselves how well they followed the rules. A simple anecdotal observation form (such as Form 31) is one

way for teachers to evaluate student performance, and a student check sheet (Form 32) will direct students' self-evaluations. Simply write a classroom rule on each line and let students rate themselves.

Work together with parents. During all phases of rules instruction, it is helpful to include students' families in the process. Providing parents with information, asking for their help in checking homework, and involving them in the evaluation process will help students understand and value the rules. Students will also see that home and school are going to work together to foster consistently appropriate behavior. Form 33 is a sample letter that you could send to parents. Form 34 is a parent checkup sheet on homework practice. Have each of your students fill in the top part of the form, then send it home to parents.

Make seating charts easier to keep. Get a manila folder and put small sticky notes on the inside to represent the chair or table arrangement in your classroom. Write each student's name on a sticky note to represent his/her seat. When you change seats, just move the sticky notes. You don't need to rewrite a plan or to erase. This saves time when you are moving several students.

easy seating charts

Forms
for
Chapter
6

form 22 Sample Rule Teaching Guide

Physical Aggression

- Rule: Physical aggression is not allowed.

- Short Forms: No fighting, no hitting, no biting, no hurting others

- Rationale: School should be a safe place. We don't do anything that could physically harm anyone.

- Definition: Physical aggression is any behavior that could harm someone (including yourself). It usually means that a person actively does something aggressive to someone else. However, you could also do something indirectly or covertly that could cause harm. Some examples include: (1) Not informing someone of danger (e.g., telling someone to do something that you know is dangerous); (2) Getting someone to commit an aggressive act for you (e.g., getting one student to beat up another); or (3) Doing something that has a subsequent dangerous effect (e.g., giving someone a dangerous object to use or play with).

- Some Examples of Physical Aggression:
    - Hitting, kicking, fighting, or wrestling
    - Biting, scratching, or spitting
    - Throwing things
    - Running when walking is required
    - Self-abuse
    - Having or sharing weapons or other dangerous objects
    - Encouraging others to do something dangerous, such as fighting or running

- Positive Examples:
    - Keeping hands and feet to yourself
    - Walking when moving around in the classroom and other school areas
    - Avoiding fights
    - Using words instead of actions
    - Ignoring provocations or teasing
    - Walking away from an argument

form 23

Just a Reminder!

Be a good friend.

form 24

Keep your hands to yourself.

form 25

Be where you are

supposed to be.

form 26 Sample Rules Test

Name: _____ Date: _____

Rule: Do not say mean things

Place an X beside each example of a nice thing to say.

_____   1. You are stupid!

_____   2. Will you sit by me at lunch today?

_____   3. It's all your fault!

_____   4. I'm going to get you for that!

_____   5. Come play with us!

_____   6. Will you shut up?

_____   7. That is a pretty dress.

_____   8. My picture is better than yours.

_____   9. That is a great picture!

_____   10. Will you show me how to play the game?

form 27 Sample Rules Test

Name: _____Date: _____

Teacher: _____

1. What are the rules in this class? List them.

    A. _____

    B. _____

    C. _____

    D. _____

    E. _____

2. For each rule listed above, give an example of a behavior that breaks the rule.

    A. _____

    B. _____

    C. _____

    D. _____

    E. _____

3. Why do you think the teacher has these particular rules? _____

4. If a student did each of the following, which rules (list the letters from above) would he/she be breaking?

_____ cursing	_____ arguing	_____ talking out
_____ sleeping in class	_____ using drugs	_____ threatening
_____ making disruptive or inappropriate noises	_____ spitting	_____ stealing
_____ hitting someone	_____ lying	_____ destroying property
_____ talking back	_____ being late	_____ throwing food
_____ bossing people	_____ burping	_____ wearing cap in school

(cont'd)

form 27 (cont'd)

5. What are the consequences (penalties or punishments) for breaking the rules?

_____
_____
_____

6. Do you think the consequences used to enforce the rules are fair or unfair?

_____
_____
_____

Why?_____
_____
_____

7. What consequences for breaking the rules do you dislike the most?

_____
_____
_____

form 28 Student Rule Following Agreement

Use this form to help a student follow a specific classroom rule. Setting up a contract like this will keep the student focused. Both you and the student should agree on a positive consequence and evaluation date, then sign where indicated.

I will practice: _____

_____
Student

If I do, then: _____

_____

_____
Teacher

_____
Date

To be reevaluated on or before: _____
Date

form 29 Homework Assignment for Rules

Student:_____

Rule:_____

Definition:_____

Please discuss this rule with your child, and help him/her to list three ways to follow this rule in the classroom. This assignment is due tomorrow with your signature. Thank you for your help!

1. _____

_____

_____

2. _____

_____

_____

3. _____

_____

_____

Parent's Signature: _____

form 3o Sample Floor Plan

Study Carrels

Quiet Area

Supply Cabinets/Counter

Optional
Activities Area

Low Bookshelves

TV/VCR

Blackboard

Large Group
Instruction Area

Blackboard

Bookshelf

Small
Group
Instruction
Area

Bookshelves or Blackboard

Bookshelf

Reading
Area

Soft Chairs

Carpet

Bulletin Board

Teacher/Assistant
Area

Bookshelf/Files

form 3 1 Anecdotal Observation of Rule Following

In the left column, list the classroom rules. Along the top row, name the students or groups being observed. Then use checks (3) or tally marks (///) to record instances when the rules are being followed.

Observer: _____Date:_____

Rules Being Observed	Student or Group	Student or Group	Student or Group	Student or Group

form 32 Student Check Sheet on Rule Following

Name: _____Date:_____

Class: _____

How often did you follow these rules? (Circle one)

Rule 1:

_____

Never   Sometimes   Always

Rule 2:

_____

Never   Sometimes   Always

Rule 3:

_____

Never   Sometimes   Always

form 33 Sample Letter to Parent

Dear Parent,

Your child is working to learn the rules of _____ grade. We will be discussing these rules in class during the following week. In order to ensure that each student and parent has a full understanding of these rules, I am asking you to discuss these rules with your child at home. Each night, he/she will be given a written homework assignment to be completed and returned to school with your signature. Please help your child complete these assignments. If you have any questions, feel free to contact me at _____. Thank you for your help in ensuring that our students have a safe and happy year!

                    Thank you,

                    Teacher's Signature _____

Examples of Classroom Rules

- Make positive and encouraging comments.

- Follow the teacher's directions.

- Respect others' property.

- Be where you are supposed to be.

- Be an independent learner.

form 34 Parent Checkup on Rules Homework

Dear Parent:

Please circle one of the three faces to indicate how well your child did on following the rule at home. Thanks for your help.

Teacher's Signature:_____

Name: _____ Date: _____

Rule:_____

When_____ practiced the rule, here's how he/she did:

set up a "user-friendly" system of consequences

When misbehavior occurs, it is best to respond to it systematically and consistently.

When students behave cooperatively and are engaged in learning, teaching is fun and rewarding. However, when students are uncooperative or disruptive, or they challenge your authority, less learning takes place and everyone may be discouraged and unhappy. Establishing a clear system of consequences and using it consistently can have a powerful, positive effect on teaching and learning.

Chapter **7**

What to Do and How to Do it

1 Begin to think about an overall plan.

Recognize the value of a systematic approach. A classroom is a dynamic, interactive environment with a constant ebb and flow of activity. For teachers, whose population of students is increasingly diverse and challenging, dealing with student behavior may be the most important step in successful teaching. The list of behaviors that are critical for school success seems endless.

Students must listen to and follow instructions, remain on-task, complete assignments, maintain interpersonal relationships, deal with their and others' emotions, and work independently, just to name a few. These skills and many others are so important in the school environment that when students fail to demonstrate them in an acceptable and appropriate manner, it may become almost impossible to teach or learn. We have previously discussed desirable, prosocial behaviors that we hope students demonstrate in school. Unfortunately, however, students

also demonstrate behaviors that are not desirable, pleasant, cooperative, or helpful to the teaching/learning process. You must be prepared to respond quickly and successfully to these disruptive behaviors if you hope to maintain a safe, orderly, and positive climate for learning.

Plan to focus on prevention. Prevention of behavior problems is a good strategy for several reasons. First, it keeps you on a positive track. It's usually less stressful and more appealing to prevent problems than to react

141

to them. Second, preventive strategies often result in a more favorable environment for learning. When students are behaving appropriately in class, they often attend more to your instruction. Third, prevention can result in reduction of many different behaviors, not just one that has become a serious problem. When you establish a positive climate and a clear, consistent set of consequences, students may be less likely to present their entire repertoire of undesirable behaviors because they understand that the consequences will apply to any disruptive behavior. Planning ahead, responding quickly and early in a pattern of misbehavior, and encouraging students to learn appropriate behaviors are some of the ways that you can make your system work effectively.

2 Establish your behavioral continuum.

Prioritize problem behaviors. It is impossible to respond to every incident of misbehavior that occurs in a classroom. Therefore, you need to think about what's most important in your particular class. Decide which behaviors are the most serious infractions of community, school district, and administration rules. Consider your own personal limits, and what you deem acceptable and appropriate in the classroom. Then, begin to arrange students' behavior problems by rank, ordering them in terms

of severity. Use Form 35 as a tool, filling it in as you decide which student behaviors are a concern to you and how serious a problem each behavior is. After undesirable behaviors have been ranked by how disruptive, inappropriate, or socially unacceptable they are, you will be able to design consequences that vary along a similar continuum, from least to most intensive.

Group similar types of behaviors together. Another strategy for deciding how serious some behaviors are is categorizing. Try grouping similar behaviors together in a framework similar to that on Form 36. When you categorize behaviors according to their most likely responses, you have made several decisions, including which behaviors are most important, which behaviors have the most serious negative effects in the classroom, and the typical responses to these disturbing behaviors. Filling out this grid requires thoughtful consideration, and the process will guide you in selecting appropriate consequences.

"You don't have a problem; you just have a decision to make."

Robert Schuller

---

3 Evaluate your beliefs about the use of consequences for misbehavior.

Recognize the need for consequences. We have already discussed the use of positive reinforcement as a strategy for increasing desirable behaviors. For many reasons already described, positive reinforcement is our preferred option for dealing with students' behaviors in the classroom. Nevertheless, when misbehavior is dangerous, disruptive, or likely to escalate, other strategies, including punishment, may sometimes be necessary. For many of us, the use of punishment is problematic. Research has sometimes disputed the long-term effectiveness of punishment, and there are limitations to punishment as a strategy for changing behavior. Nevertheless, misbehavior that requires consequences can and will occur in the classroom. So, just as consequences are used in society when an individual's behavior violates our legal, ethical, and moral standards, consequences are also part of the organizational and governance structure of schools. This chapter will discuss consequences that may be used in school as natural, logical responses to misbehavior. We will not include a discussion of corporal or physical punishment, nor do we advocate its use in school.

S ome of the most effective consequences are the ones that students expect least.
For example, try:

- Waiting quietly for attention
- Letting a student choose his/her own consequence
- Moving either your location or the student's
- Lowering (instead of raising) your voice

try unexpected consequences

Consider new choices of consequences.

In a previous discussion of positive reinforcement, we presented some ways to select effective reinforcers. We mentioned that teachers can inadvertently choose positive reinforcers that have little impact on students' behavior. The same is true of consequences intended to decrease the occurrence of a behavior. We are sometimes so rooted in tradition that we continue to use consequences that have been a part of school culture for years, even when they have little significance to students and do not change behavior. When a consequence is not an effective deterrent and therefore fails to decrease the occurrence of a behavior, other consequences should be considered. Here are several guidelines for choosing the most effective consequences:

- Choose consequences that are respectful of students and their families.

- Have a variety of consequences available from several categories, including:

  – Reprimands
  – Loss of privileges
  – Apology and/or restitution
  – Changes in routines or procedures
  – Community/school service
  – Participation in group or individual behavior-changing activities
  – Problem solving
  – Parent contact
  – Referral to other professionals

- Be clear in your own mind about which consequences you are and are not comfortable with.

- Don't choose consequences about which you have legal, ethical, or moral reservations.

- Whenever possible, ask students for their ideas and suggestions for appropriate consequences.

4 Generate an extensive menu of consequences.

Brainstorm to create a list of ideas. The next step in designing a system of consequences is to think of all of the possible consequences you have available to you. One process that is helpful is brainstorming. We use brainstorming when we want to generate a large quantity or long list of ideas, usually ideas that are solutions to problems. To help you develop a wide variety of interesting and effective consequences, include fellow teachers and instructional assistants, students, parents, consultants, administrators, and related services personnel in the brainstorming group. Before you begin, consider the ages of your students, their typical behavior patterns, interventions that have already been attempted, students' responses to specific individuals, and any other related variables. Then, follow the simple procedure outlined here:

- Assemble a brainstorming group consisting of about five to ten people.

- Choose at least one person to record the group's ideas.

- Set a timer for ten minutes.

- Discuss these guidelines: The purpose of brainstorming is to generate a large number of ideas. Ideas should not be discussed, evaluated, praised, or criticized during the brainstorming session. Those things can be done later, during the evaluation and discussion session. Also, everyone should participate.

- Begin.

  – Think of as many consequences as you can for students' misbehaviors.
  – Try to think of novel and original ideas.
  – Have the recorder(s) write each idea down.
  – Continue until the timer goes off.

- After the brainstorming period ends, evaluate.

  – Eliminate duplicate ideas, discuss advantages and disadvantages of each consequence, and write a final list of options.

Collect ideas from other sources. There are many excellent sources for information about discipline and behavior management. After you have worked with your own team or school-based group, you may also wish to consult other professionals. There are books, curricula, video training systems, and journal articles that can provide helpful information about how to implement a

system of consequences for student behavior. Collect copies, notes, descriptions, and random ideas in a folder, then read through everything you have collected, eliminating ideas that are impractical for you or that you don't feel comfortable with. Next, decide which ideas you can use as they are and which ones you can adapt and modify to fit your own personal style and situation. Keep in mind that lots of great class-wide management plans, token economies, and consequence systems have already been developed, so it is not always necessary for you to start at the very beginning.

5 Develop a continuum of consequences.

Prioritize your list of consequences. Just as you ranked students' disruptive and undesirable behaviors from least to most serious, do the same for your consequences. First, list those consequences that are nonverbal. Continue to add more intrusive and intensive consequences to your list, so that when you are finished, you have a continuum ranging from mild to severe. A sample continuum of consequences is presented following, and you can use Form 37 to design your own. Your continuum will help you make decisions about appropriate consequences, so that you do not overreact to minor infractions or ignore major ones.

Try a "response cost" strategy instead of a more traditional punishment. This technique involves distributing tokens, points, coupons, tickets, or other items in an equal number to all students. Students give up one item each time they demonstrate a specific misbehavior (like talking out or failing to stay on-task). Students who have a specified number of items left at the end of the period, day, etc. are allowed to enter their names in a raffle, participate in an activity, or continue with a group game.

response cost

Least Intensive

- A "look" from teacher
- Teacher proximity (moving in and standing close)
- Non-verbal signal (flashing the room lights, orange signal card, etc.)
- Verbal reminder of rule
- Verbal reprimand/warning
- Loss of a point or check in monitoring system
- Change of seat
- Loss of privilege:
    - Recess
    - Class helper role
    - Preferred activity
- Response to tape-recorded questions on rules
- Written exercise:
    - Explain rules
    - Copy rules
    - Explain behavior
- Seating restriction at lunch
- Individual conference with the teacher
- Complete a problem-solving exercise
- Cool-down time at desk with head down
- Time-out in other area of the classroom or in outside area
- Student telephone call to parent(s)
- Restitution
- Referral to discipline team of students and/or teachers
- Teacher telephone call or note to parent(s)
- Referral to counselor or administrator

Most Intensive

sample continuum of consequences

Consider using consequences that are non-verbal, like signals, body position, and facial expressions. Non-verbal responses to student misbehavior are unobtrusive, easy to use, and effective. They do not interrupt the flow of your teaching, and they do not draw a lot of attention to the student offender.

non-verbal responses

Decide which consequences you will use with which behaviors. It is best to narrow your final continuum down to between four and seven consequences, or better still, to have two different continuums, one for minor misbehaviors and one for more serious behavior problems. Students have such a diverse repertoire of behaviors that it would be unrealistic to have a different set of consequences for each specific misbehavior that occurs in the classroom. Choose the consequences that you believe to be most effective, most in tune with your teaching style, most appropriate for your students' ages and ability levels, and easiest to use for a variety of misbehaviors. Also consider the number of consequences in your continuum. Having too many steps may allow students' misbehavior to continue so long that it escalates. Too few steps may not provide ample opportunities for students to regain control of their behavior. Form 38 will help you compile your final list of consequences for specific behaviors. This final plan can be taught to students, posted in the classroom, and referred to as a teaching tool whenever necessary.

6 Implement your plan.

Teach your class about the continuum. After you have written your continuum and your plan, teach your students what the consequences are and how they will be implemented. Teach the consequences the same way you taught the rules (see Chapter 6), using a systematic approach like the one used for academic instruction. Take the time to specify objectives, introduce concepts, provide examples, role play, practice the procedures, allow for questions, and give feedback. Make sure everyone is clear about when, how, and why the consequences will be implemented. You may also want to display posters in your classroom to advise students of consequences. Form 39 shows a sample poster design.

Use your consequences the way you planned. If your consequences are well-considered, reasonable, and clear to students, there should be little confusion when you begin to implement them. Consistency is very important. The consequences that you have chosen should be used with each student after each occurrence of misbehavior. Try not to threaten, repeat warnings, or allow students to talk you out of a consequence. The sooner students learn that you will be consistent, the sooner the consequences will start to be effective. It is also a good idea to implement consequences in a matter-of-fact style, without anger or excitement. Causing teachers to "lose their cool" and become visibly angry or upset can be very strong positive reinforcement for some students. If they learn that the consequence for a certain behavior is that the teacher looks foolish or is out of control, behavior will likely increase in frequency. Some practical guidelines for implementing consequences are suggested here:

- Make sure everyone knows the consequence for each behavior.

  – If you or the students are not sure, take the time to clarify.
  – Inform parents and others who need to know.

- Follow through with a consequence after each misbehavior.

  – Don't give second chances.
  – Don't continue to warn.

- Be consistent.

  – If you have explained a consequence, use it.
  – Don't change your mind after the behavior has occurred.

- Just do it.

  – The time for talking and explaining is before the misbehavior.
  – Go ahead and use your consequences without a lot of discussion.

- Stay cool.

  – Don't get angry and upset; just follow your plan.

  – If you do get angry and upset, try not to show it.

- Don't feel guilty.

  – If your consequences are fair and consistent, there's no reason to feel guilty.
  – Remind yourself that if you tolerate and condone misbehavior, your students may suffer worse consequences later.

7 Evaluate your system.

Observe what happens. The best way to determine whether your consequences are working is to watch the students' behavior. After you have used your system for a reasonable length of time (about two to three weeks), evaluate its effectiveness. If the misbehavior continues and/or increases in frequency or intensity, then your

---

Try this consequence system for elementary students. Choose two of your classroom rules to use with the system, for example:

- Sit in your desk during seatwork time.
- Raise your hand and wait for permission to talk.

Start your class each day with the word "RECESS" written in big letters across the top of the board. Each time you have to reprimand students for being out of their seats or talking without permission, erase a letter. If students have to be reprimanded six or more times, the word disappears and so does their recess.

don't let our recess disappear

consequences may not be effective. Just as you should evaluate your systems of rules and positive reinforcement, you should keep track of students' behavior so that you know if the consequences for misbehavior have the intended effect. Be objective, collect data (see Chapter 8) that are reliable and accurate, ask for an outside observer, and elicit feedback from students.

If things aren't working, make adjustments. If your consequences do not have the desired impact, go back to the previous steps in the chapter. Examine your priorities, brainstorm some additional consequences, and add to or delete from your continuum. The nice thing about plans is that they can be changed. Throughout this chapter, we have included some unusual and creative

consequences that vary from traditional responses. For more complete systems that integrate rules, positive reinforcement, behavior monitoring, and consequences, refer to Chapter 11.

Forms
for
Chapter

7

form 35 Misbehavior: From Bad to Worse

Behaviors That Are Unacceptable in This Class

Little Problems:
_____
_____
_____
_____
_____

Medium Problems:
_____
_____
_____
_____
_____

Big Problems:
_____
_____
_____
_____
_____

form 36 What's the Behavior? What's the Plan?

Behaviors I will try to prevent with
rules/reminders:

_____

_____

_____

Behaviors I will consequate myself:

_____

_____

_____

Behaviors that will involve others
(parents/consultants):

_____

_____

_____

Behaviors requiring extreme interventions (e.g., police/crisis team):

_____

_____

_____

Which of these behaviors are
most likely to respond to a positive reinforcement plan?

_____

_____

_____

form 37 My Continuum of Consequences

Least Intensive Consequences

1 _____

2 _____

3 _____

4 _____

5 _____

6 _____

7 _____

8 _____

Most Intensive Consequences

form 38 What's the Behavior? What's the Response?

Student Behavior	Teacher Response
If you do this:	Then this will happen:
If you do this:	Then this will happen:

form 39

If You Interrupt Teaching or Learning

First, I'll signal you, THEN it's conference time!

monitor behavior simply and efficiently

Close, consistent monitoring of student behavior enables teachers to evaluate students' progress and to plan for instruction.

When teachers monitor students' behavior effectively and accurately, they can diagnose problems quickly. Then, activities can be designed either to remediate behavior or to extend learning. Close monitoring can provide objective data, which help teachers, administrators, parents, students, and others to make decisions about students' progress and placement, and about necessary supports and modifications to classroom/school procedures.

Chapter

8

What to Do and How to Do it

1 Decide what you need from a monitoring system.

Be clear about why you may want to monitor behavior. There are several reasons to closely monitor students' behavior. In schools today, there are many students whose behavior problems are seriously disruptive or who lack the social/behavioral skills necessary to work well with others. In addition, increased inclusion of students with disabilities into general education classrooms almost guarantees that all teachers will, at some point, have students in their classrooms with behavior problems. Close monitoring can be of great benefit to teachers and administrators, especially when it is designed to:

- Provide clear information to use as a basis for referral and placement decisions

- Provide specific documentation that educators can share with students' families

- Give teachers feedback that can help them decide if their interventions are having a positive effect on students' behaviors

- Help students begin to focus on the behaviors that are being monitored, often encouraging students to self-monitor, self-evaluate, and improve their self-control

- Encourage objectivity by clarifying exactly what is expected of the student and how he/she will be evaluated in measurable terms

Close observation and monitoring are often the first steps in developing a successful strategy for changing student behavior. Without the data provided by a monitoring system, teacher interventions might have to rely on more subjective information like "hunches," guesses, or feelings. These intuitive conclusions may be less accurate, because teachers are not just detached observers but participants with a vested interest in what happens in the classroom.

Think about what is most important to you. It is helpful to be clear about your criteria before designing your behavior monitoring system. Consider your personal style, your students' ages and abilities, and the structure of your class and school. For example, most teachers would probably say that they want a monitoring system that is easy, quick, and simple to use. Mrs. Fisher may think that "simple" means spending 30 seconds once per day to circle a number on a card. Mr. Giles may be interested in rating ten different behaviors on a scale of 1-4, then spending 20 minutes adding up points and calculating a percentage. Think about how much time and effort you would like to spend monitoring behavior, then consider any other criteria you think are relevant. Answering the following questions may help you decide on a system that will meet your individual needs:

- Do I want a system for my entire class, or one for individual students?

- How much time do I want to spend monitoring behavior (how much time per class period, per day, per week, etc.)?

- Will I do all the work, or will the students and/or other adults help me?

- What instruments will my students be willing to use?

- How complicated should my system be? Do I want to make special considerations for some categories of behaviors or some specific times of day?

- Do I want to monitor how my students perform in other classes besides my own?

- How will I involve parents? Will I work with them on designing the system and/or on using it?

- Have I seen a system that I can modify to fit my needs?

- Do I want to count specific behaviors as they occur, or do I want to use a general, overall rating?

- Will my monitoring system be related to student incentives (rewards, privileges, etc.)? Do I want to tie it in with a more extensive management system?

2 Collect input and advice.

Gather relevant information. One way to collect information about monitoring systems is to gather examples of systems that others use. There are many excellent materials available today that provide the basics of monitoring systems. It is neither necessary nor efficient to write or design something that has already been done. Looking at other teachers' monitoring strategies can help you develop ideas of your own and/or provide you with systems to use "as is." Forms 40-42 are examples of various monitoring forms to give you ideas. Your choice of materials should reflect your individual needs and should meet the criteria you have already identified.

Consult other professionals. Many teachers have access to the expertise of consultants, helping or consulting teachers, student intervention/assistance teams, mentors, or master teachers. Teachers also have grade-level or academic team members, department cohorts, and friends and acquaintances on their campuses. Take advantage of whatever resources are available. Sign up for staff development training, ask questions, look at professional books and magazines for ideas, observe in other classrooms, and ask for help from your colleagues and family. You never know who may have a simple idea that you would never think of on your own.

Ask your students and their parents for assistance. In Chapter 6, we discussed reasons and ways to involve your students in developing your classroom rules. Students can also suggest ways in which they can be evaluated on following those rules. Depending on your decision-making style, you may want to make all final decisions yourself, allow a vote on some issues, or limit student participation to advice only. Regardless of how much input you allow your students, listening to their ideas and suggestions before you design a monitoring strategy might prevent mistakes and time-consuming changes later. When considering implementation of any monitoring system, it is also a good idea to talk to your students' parents. They can tell you what they would be willing to

do, including whether they would like to examine a daily report and sign it, follow up with behavioral "homework," or reinforce with privileges at home.

3 Now, design a written monitoring form to fit your needs.

First, choose your target behaviors. Select behaviors to monitor that are most important to you and your students. These behaviors might include following your classroom rules, students' goals from their IEPs, or behaviors that have become disruptive or intolerable. For young students and students with serious behavioral problems, focus on one to three critical behaviors; for older students, five to ten behaviors can sometimes be monitored easily. State your target behaviors positively if you can; that is, say what to do instead of what not to do. Also, use action verbs so that you can observe and measure easily. For example, "Raise your hand before talking" is both

observable and easy to count. If you must focus on eliminating a behavior, try to make the behavior definition as clear as possible. ("No hitting others.")

Second, decide how often you want to record students' behaviors. For young students, you might want to monitor every half hour; for older students, checking up at the end of each class period may be more convenient. If you are focusing on a severely disruptive or continual behavior, monitor more often.

Third, establish some monitoring guidelines so that recording is done consistently and fairly. When more than one student is being monitored, or when more than one adult is evaluating and recording, students will pay careful attention to see that the same standards are applied to each of them in an equitable manner. One easy way to maintain consistency is to record reprimands. For example, if Tim behaves appropriately without your reprimanding or warning him, he will earn three points on his Daily Report Form (Form 40). However, if you must warn him about misbehavior, you will put one slash mark (/) in the appropriate box on his form and he will receive only two points. If he requires two warnings, you will put two slashes on his form (//) and he will only earn a 1. This way, students know the exact criteria for earning a particular number of points, and they also receive some immediate feedback that might help them modify their behavior before it continues too long.

Fourth, choose the numerical or symbolic system for your recording form. Sometimes you can use hole punches (Form 41). You can also use + or − marks (Form 42). Some monitoring forms call for a simple "yes" or "no" and others involve number ratings (from 0-4 or from 1-3). Regardless of the system, be as clear as possible about your criteria for earning the desired score or symbol. Using Form 19 from Chapter 5 may help students to be sure of your standards.

Next, create a sample version of your form on paper. Share it with any other adults who may be monitoring with you. Ask yourselves these questions:

● Is the form easy to read?

● Are the directions clear?

● Should we use regular paper or do we need to laminate the form or use card stock?

● Is the design appealing and attractive to students (illustrations, typeface, etc.)?

● Is the time required to compute a score for each student reasonable?

● Will parents understand what the form means and how to evaluate their child's performance?

Finally, clarify your procedures for using the monitoring form. Make sure students, teachers, and assistants all understand how often and by whom students' behavior will be monitored. Also discuss the verbal reinforcement that you will use as you record a point, punch the card, or stamp the paper. Using specific praise as you monitor each behavior will make the process more effective. If the monitoring record will be tied into a reinforcement system that involves tokens, play money, or tangible reinforcers, be sure that everyone is clear how this will work (see Chapter 11).

4 Make preparations to implement your system.

Plan out a step-by-step approach for implementation. Change is sometimes difficult. When you implement a behavior monitoring system, take the time to prepare yourself and your students. Rushing into something before everyone is ready may result in wasting time later in order to revise, reteach, explain, or answer questions. Monitoring behavior is just like any other teaching activity; it works better when you plan and prepare for it. If you introduce the system slowly, you may also avoid some of the resistance that those involved may feel about making a change.

Establish a schedule for evaluating. Set some dates to evaluate how well the system is working. Plan an initial problem-solving session, perhaps at the end of the first week. This session should focus on the logistics of the system, including ease of administration and students', understanding of the system. Plan, also, to check on the consistency among the adults who are monitoring. Compare information with each other to see if you agree on which behaviors meet criteria and which do not. Also, set a date for a more long-range evaluation of student progress. The end of a six-week grading period is an obvious time to evaluate how well students are performing and whether the monitoring system is effective and efficient. Plan to present and evaluate data at that time on individual students, specific behaviors, and overall class progress.

5 Teach everyone the behavior monitoring system.

Make sure *you* understand your system. Take time to review your written form. One way to ensure your own understanding is to practice explaining the system to someone else. Find a friend who is willing to pose as a student. Then, using the monitoring form for reference, role play your explanation.

Work through a simulated class with the "student." Then ask for questions and suggestions. The questions in the following box are useful, because they permit you to consider situations that you may not have anticipated.

Teach the system to the other adults who will use it. Once you are clear about what you're doing and how, it's time to teach the others involved. First, share your information with any administrators who may be involved in supervising or monitoring your class. It is important that they have an understanding of any new monitoring system, since behavior may change when the consequences change. Next, teach the assistants, co-teachers, monitors, and anyone else who will be directly involved with the system. Focus special attention on those individuals who will work with you to monitor behavior and record information. Use the procedure suggested previously, role playing all possible scenarios. It is critical that all adults involved be thoroughly familiar with the procedures, because students will very quickly look for inconsistencies or ways to "get around" your system. Again, decide on responses to the questions in this box and listen to constructive suggestions.

Teach the students about the system.
Once all of the adults involved are clear and confident, teach the students how their behavior will be monitored. Use adult models to explain and demonstrate. Provide students with

samples of monitoring forms, so that they can follow your presentation. Then, have the students role play, simulating a typical class period. After the modeling and role play, allow discussion and questions. If everyone understands the procedures, there is a greater chance that implementation will be smooth and consistent. After teaching the system, check students' understanding with either an oral or a written evaluation, including questions like those listed in the box. (These can be modified or adapted to fit your needs.) Next, make plans to practice the procedures regularly. With young students, you may need a five-minute session at the beginning of each school day for the first few weeks, then a weekly or monthly

review. Older students will also require review and practice, hopefully less often (perhaps once per week, then once or twice each semester).

6 Put the system into practice.

Watch for behavior changes. When you begin to closely monitor student behavior in a systematic way, several things may happen. Sometimes, student behavior can deteriorate briefly, especially if some undesirable student behaviors were receiving lots of teacher attention before, and now result only in observation, brief reprimand, or a written comment on a form. The

Ask students the following questions to test for understanding:
- What are the goals of this system?
- What specific behaviors are we going to monitor in our classroom?
- Who is going to check and record your behavior?
- What steps will we follow to check and record your behavior?
- How many points (checks, punches, tickets, etc.) can you earn?
- How can we tell how many points (checks, punches, tickets, etc.) to award? For example, what are the criteria for unacceptable, acceptable, or outstanding behavior?
- What are your responsibilities regarding the recording form?
- What are your parents' responsibilities regarding the recording form?

do your students understand your monitoring system?

teacher attention was reinforcing, and the student may intensify the behavior in order to try to receive the reinforcement again.

On the other hand, student behavior may improve rapidly and consistently, simply due to the observation. Either way, keeping good written records will help you make decisions about students' behavioral progress.

"Adopt the pace of nature; her secret is patience."   Emerson

---

Stick with the plan, but don't be afraid to refine it. Teacher interventions for student behavior will work best when they are consistent. Therefore, once you have designed and implemented a good behavior monitoring system, stick with it long enough to allow it to produce positive results. Many teachers suggest continuing a

new plan for a minimum of two to three weeks. This seems to be enough time for new habits to develop, kinks to work out of the system, and change to begin. However, while maintaining your consistent approach, don't be afraid to fine-tune your system. Regular evaluation sessions that examine the system's effectiveness will provide critical information. Small changes that improve the system are helpful, as long as everyone involved still understands and uses the same procedures.

7 Move toward student self-monitoring.

Begin to teach self-monitoring skills to your class. Sometimes students are not aware of what they are doing and how often they are doing it. Before students can learn to control their behavior, they must know that it is occurring. Some simple strategies for teaching students to monitor their own behavior will be explained in Chapter 15. However, this section will present basic information that will enable you to begin the process. The simplest strategy is to ask students to monitor their behavior using the same tool that you use. The record form, check sheet, or report card that you are using in your system can often be used by students. At the end of each class period or day, compare your monitoring records with

theirs. Use the comparison to teach them specific expectations, examples and nonexamples of specific behaviors, and alternatives to undesirable behaviors. Sometimes, the act of recording the behavior is all it takes for students to make a change.

Give students some tools. Three convenient tools are included at the end of this chapter that can help build students' self-monitoring skills. Form 43 is a variation of an idea from *Project RIDE* (1993). It uses a beeper tape to focus students' attention on their own behaviors. Form 44 helps students monitor the steps in completing academic work. Form 45 requires students to monitor how many positive and negative comments they make. You could set a goal with the student such as "more positive than negative comments," a certain ratio of positive to negative comments, or "no negative comments." Then the student could use the form to track his/her progress.

Forms
for
Chapter

8

form 40 Daily Report Form

Use this form to monitor individual students' behaviors. Each time a student requires a warning, place a small slash (/) in the appropriate box, then use the code below to award points. After determining the total number of points possible during one school day, set a criterion as a goal for the student. At the end of the day, compute the student's total, then evaluate to see if the criterion has been met.

Name: _____　　　　　　Date: _____

Point Codes:　0 = Noncompliant (3 or more warnings given)
1 = Needs Improvement (2 warnings given)
2 = Satisfactory (1 warning given)
3 = Excellent (Performed beyond what was required)

				Class P	eriods					
	1	2	3	4	5	6	7	Daily Totals	Comments	
Class Rules/Behavior Problems										
1. Physical Aggression										
2. Verbal Abuse										
3. Unacceptable Social Behavior										
4. Disruptions										
5. Not Getting Along										
IEP Skills/Social Skills										
1.										
2.										
3.										
4.										
5.										
Academics										
1. Preparation										
2. Following Directions										
3. On-Task										
4. Task Completion										
5. Task Completion Quality										
Involvement										
1. Attention										
2. Demonstrating Interest/Asking Questions										
3. Self-Evaluation										
4. Cooperation										
5. Helping Others										
Class Period Totals								Grand Total Earned		

Total Satisfactory Points Possible:_____　Points Needed for 80% Criterion:_____　Total Points Earned:_____　Criteria Met: Yes ❏ No ❏

form 41 Sample Punch Card

Give each student a punch card like the one here. Walk around the classroom on a random schedule. When you see a student displaying a target behavior, verbally praise him/her and use a hole-puncher to punch the student's card. (As an added bonus, you could allow students to punch their own cards.)

Give each student a reward when all the holes on his/her card are punched. If students agree to the idea, display the completed cards on a bulletin board. For variety, give the entire class a party or other group reward after everyone's card is completely punched.

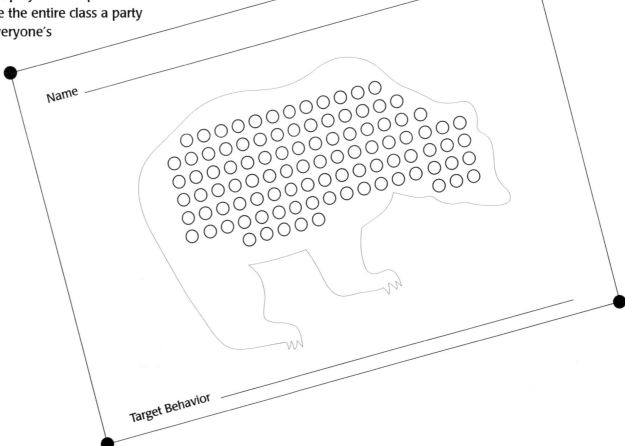

Name _____

Target Behavior _____

form 42 Paying Attention

The adult should fill in the times during which "attending" is important. Times can be entered in small increments (e.g. five minutes) for high-attention work, or for longer increments (e.g., one hour) for tasks during which attention needs to be less concentrated. Either the student or the adult can put a "+" for times when attention is appropriate and a "−" for times when the student is inattentive.

TIME	MON	TUES	WED	THURS	FRI
TOTALS					

Name: _____ Week Of: _____ Total Score for Week:_____

form 43 Am I Working?

Use this form in combination with a beeper tape (an audiotape on which audible "beeps" have been recorded using a doorbell or chime). This system is designed for use with an individual student, and is especially helpful for improving on-task behavior. Each time the beep sounds, the student is to ask himself/herself, "Am I working?" and record a + or − mark on the form. The beeps can be recorded at either regular or irregular intervals, and they can be very frequent (every two minutes) or less frequent (every 15 minutes), depending on the student's age, prior instruction, and stage of mastery. As they first learn the procedure, students can ask the question aloud. Gradually, they should be instructed to ask themselves the question silently and internally, as they would for many behaviors requiring self-monitoring and self-control.

YES	NO

Adapted with permission from Great Falls Public Schools (1993). *Project RIDE: Responding to individual differences in education (Elementary version)*. Longmont, CO: Sopris West. All rights reserved.

form 44 Work Completion

Student:_____ Week of: _____

Period Subject	MON	TUES	WED	THURS	FRI
I wrote down the assignment.					
I began the assignment.					
I completed the assignment.					
I turned in the assignment.					
Period Subject	MON	TUES	WED	THURS	FRI
I wrote down the assignment.					
I began the assignment.					
I completed the assignment.					
I turned in the assignment.					
Period Subject	MON	TUES	WED	THURS	FRI
I wrote down the assignment.					
I began the assignment.					
I completed the assignment.					
I turned in the assignment.					
Period Subject	MON	TUES	WED	THURS	FRI
I wrote down the assignment.					
I began the assignment.					
I completed the assignment.					
I turned in the assignment.					
Period Subject	MON	TUES	WED	THURS	FRI
I wrote down the assignment.					
I began the assignment.					
I completed the assignment.					
I turned in the assignment.					

I will put an "X" in the box if nothing was assigned or due during that period. When a box is successfully completed, I will initial that box.

I will meet with _____ to discuss my progress. When/Where:_____

When I have _____ boxes filled in (including those marked with an "X") I will earn _____.

I also recognize that when I have _____ boxes filled in, my grades will begin to improve and I will feel very responsible.

form 45 Self-Monitoring Form

Name: _____ Week of: _____

Circle one number each time you make a comment.

Date: _____

Negative Comments	1	2	3	4	5	6	7	8	9	10	11	12	13	14	15
Positive Comments	1	2	3	4	5	6	7	8	9	10	11	12	13	14	15

Date: _____

Negative Comments	1	2	3	4	5	6	7	8	9	10	11	12	13	14	15
Positive Comments	1	2	3	4	5	6	7	8	9	10	11	12	13	14	15

Date: _____

Negative Comments	1	2	3	4	5	6	7	8	9	10	11	12	13	14	15
Positive Comments	1	2	3	4	5	6	7	8	9	10	11	12	13	14	15

Date: _____

Negative Comments	1	2	3	4	5	6	7	8	9	10	11	12	13	14	15
Positive Comments	1	2	3	4	5	6	7	8	9	10	11	12	13	14	15

Date: _____

Negative Comments	1	2	3	4	5	6	7	8	9	10	11	12	13	14	15
Positive Comments	1	2	3	4	5	6	7	8	9	10	11	12	13	14	15

take a time-out when someone needs a breather

When misbehavior becomes serious, a "time-out" will help to calm you and your students.

Incidents of serious misbehavior have become increasingly common in public schools. These behaviors include arguing, defying authority, cursing, threats and intimidation, physical aggression, and other acts that are disruptive and dangerous. It is important to de-escalate these behaviors before a crisis occurs. One of the most effective ways to de-escalate behavior is to use a time-out procedure.

Chapter 9

What to Do and How to Do it

1 Consider that things may occasionally get rough, despite your best efforts.

Recognize the need for unique interventions. In Chapter 7, we suggested writing out a continuum of behaviors, listing them in order by their levels of severity. The system of consequences that you worked out for your classroom should be sufficient for most situations. However, there are some behaviors (such as those mentioned in this chapter's Corner Piece) that are extremely serious in any context. If these serious behaviors intensify, or if they continue for a long period of time, a crisis may result. It is important to intervene before a serious behavior reaches the crisis stage. For example, an intervention should occur before the class is out of control, your authority is undermined, and/or someone is endangered. (You will find more detailed information on crises in Chapter 10.) It is also important to choose an intervention that matches the behavior, that is, one that is intensive enough to stop the behavior but not so intensive that it escalates the situation even more.

"The time to relax is when you don't have time for it."

Sydney J. Harris, contemporary educator

Begin to identify what's most problematic. By careful observation, recording, and analysis of information, you can often recognize the early signs of an impending outburst and deal with the situation effectively. Outbursts and crises sometimes follow consistent and predictable patterns. If you can identify a pattern of behavior, you may be able to prevent major problems. Pay particular attention to small, seemingly minor behaviors. These behavioral infractions are often precursors to more serious, intensive behaviors. You can use Form 46 to help you record student behavior patterns. Watch for small, infrequent behavioral infractions that follow a consistent pattern, usually leading up to more serious behaviors. When the behaviors become a consistent, predictable sequence (sometimes called a "chain" of behavior) that you can recognize, it may be possible to intervene early in the chain and prevent more serious misbehavior.

Review your continuum of consequences. Review your behavioral continuum to decide whether your interventions are early enough and strong enough. Also decide whether you are targeting the most problematic behaviors or wasting time and energy responding to less important behaviors. Dealing with behavior is a problem-solving process. If what you are doing is not working, try fine-tuning it with some minor adjustments. Changing your responses, modifying the timing of consequences, or increasing your use of positive reinforcement are all good strategies.

2 Become familiar with the concept of time-out.

Understand what time-out is. Time-out means different things to different people. Before beginning a discussion of time-out, it is a good idea to focus on one definition, so that we are clear about what we are discussing. *Time-out is a procedure in which reinforcement for a specific undesirable behavior is removed.* Always bear in mind that the regular classroom environment must be positively reinforcing to students. If it is not, or if it is more aversive than the time-out setting, then time-out will not be effective. There are several variations of time-out, which will be explained in a following section.

Understand the uses of time-out. Time-out is used commonly, but not always effectively. It is a method for responding to serious or disruptive behaviors. Proper use of time-out should cause the undesirable behavior to decrease in frequency, and eventually to disappear completely. Keep in mind that time-out is not an appropriate response to all behaviors. There are some behaviors that are so dangerous, disruptive, or psychologically damaging that responses other than time-out may be necessary. For example, bringing a weapon to school or threatening a teacher would require a more intensive consequence. However, if a student is demonstrating a consistent pattern beginning with small, irritating behaviors that continue or escalate, then time-out may be effective if

Bob Algozzine developed this strategy to use with intermediate or secondary students. It's based on the time cards used in workplaces to record employees' work time.

Find some pocket envelopes like those that used to be inside the covers of library books, or make your own. They should be 4" x 5," open at the top. Next, find some index cards that will fit into the pocket envelopes. On each card, write a student's name in large letters or paste his/her school picture. Post the envelopes on a wall or bulletin board, and put the cards into the envelopes so that names or faces are visible. When a student's behavior is escalating and he/she needs a break, "punch him/her out" by removing that student's card or turning the card to face the wall. Tell the student, "I'm punching you out for _____ minutes." While they are punched out, students don't participate in class activities, receive reinforcement, or earn privileges. This would be a good time to begin a fun activity or exciting lesson.

i'll punch you out

used early in the behavior pattern before the student has lost control. Time-out can be particularly effective for reducing behaviors that are reinforced by attention, either from you or from other students. It is also important to note that time-out should be one of the last choices on a continuum of responses, not one of the first.

3 Learn the various forms of time-out.

The following types of time-out are arranged from least to most intense.

Ignoring involves withholding adult social attention from the student for a set period of time. Examples of this technique include:

- Head Down on Desk

  This technique has been used for decades. When a student misbehaves, simply say, "Put your head down on your desk." The student then crosses his/her arms on the desktop, rests his/her forehead on them, and looks down at the desktop. During this time, the student is not allowed to talk or to make any sounds or movements, and no one should include that student in conversation.

- "I Am Ignoring You."

  Often a student will misbehave in order to gain your attention. This may occur in the form of asking too many questions, or talking out. The behaviors are not always inappropriate, but they may be too frequent, or occur at inconvenient times. After talking with the student about the attention-seeking behavior, you can institute an ignoring time-out by saying "I am ignoring you," and physically turning away from the student. You may even move some distance from the student. After 30 seconds to one minute, if the student has stopped the attention-seeking behavior you may call on him/her by saying, "Thank you for waiting for my attention; now what was your question?"

Contingent observation involves removing the student from a reinforcing group or activity to a place where he/she can continue to observe the activity but not participate in it. In gym class, coaches often use this technique when they tell a student to "sit out." Examples include:

- Time-Out Chair

  This chair is designated as the place where a student sits when given a time-out. Any type of chair can be used; however, avoid using a chair that the student might want to sit in (a bean bag chair, an overstuffed chair, etc.). The chair is placed in an isolated area in the classroom, such as a corner or in the back of the room.

- Penalty Box

  In ice hockey, when a player misbehaves, he is sent to the penalty box. This same procedure can be used in a classroom. A partition two or three feet high, and made of any material, can be placed at the side of the classroom with a chair behind it. The penalty box should be three to five feet wide and about two to three feet deep. Use a two-minute time-out with the penalty box.

Removal of materials is often used when a student is using materials inappropriately (e.g., chewing on pencils or playing with a ruler). The procedure simply involves taking the materials away from the student. Examples are:

- It's Mine Until the End of the Day

  When students are distracted by objects such as toys or other things that are forbidden at school, they are not able to focus their attention on learning, and they may misbehave or act inappropriately. After warning the student to put away the object, tell him/her, "The _____ is mine until the end of the day." Then, take away the object and put it in a secure place (e.g., a locked drawer in your desk) where it cannot be seen. Tell the student that he/she can have it at the end of the school day. He/she should also be told not to bring the object back to school.

● Bumpy Bunny

This technique was developed by Rhode, Jenson, and Reavis (1992) and is specially designed for young students. It helps avoid power struggles, because the student is not being put in time-out.

Make a space in the classroom (the top of a bookshelf is perfect) and mark it off with red tape. Each student may bring one toy of his/her choice (no toy weapons) to school to play with before class or during free time, breaks, or recess. Toys may only be brought to class on Mondays, and only one toy may be brought each week. After a week, a new toy may be brought into the classroom and the old toy returned home. Any students who exchange, sell, or lend toys lose their toy privileges for one week. Fights over toys will result in loss of toy privileges for the next day. All toys are put away (but visible on the bookshelf) during

classroom work times. If a student misbehaves, his/her toy is placed in the time-out area (the taped bookshelf area) for three to five minutes during the next play period. During this time, the student must wait at his/her desk while the other students are allowed to play. After the time-out period, the student is given the toy and is allowed to join the other students and play.

Reduction of environmental conditions

means altering the environment to remove the stimuli which allow the behavior to occur. Strategies can include:

● Covering up slick surfaces that allow objects to slip, slide, or spin

● Closing a door so sounds can't be heard

Student-controlled time-out allows a student to take a time-out when the student feels that he/she needs one. (Take care to make sure that students don't abuse this type of time-out.) This can be useful with students who feel that being sent to time-out by the teacher is embarrassing or unfair. Examples of this type of time-out are:

● The Turtle Technique

This procedure can be used with young students who act out in response to frustration. Begin by explaining that acting out often occurs in response to anger

and frustration. Then read this story to the students:

"There once was a turtle who frequently got angry in school, even though he wanted to stay calm and keep out of trouble. One day he met a wise old turtle who told him how to hide in his shell whenever he was angry. In the shell, he felt warm and comfortable, and he could rest until the angry feeling went away. The little turtle tried it the next day in school and found out that it could work for him quite well. His teacher was happy with his behavior, and everybody admired him."

After reading the story, encourage the entire class to practice the turtle technique by imagining themselves in a warm and comfortable place. Encourage them to use the technique anytime they find themselves feeling angry. When you see a student becoming angry, remind him/her to "Remember the wise old turtle."

● Technical Assistance

This method involves the use of a Technical Assistance Area (TAA), which should be located in a quiet part of the classroom away from other students and from busy areas. A four-foot square outline can be taped to the floor, or a throw rug measuring four feet on each side can be used to mark the exact area. A list of rules for the TAA should be posted there, along with a list of the three questions the student should ask himself/herself. Explain to the class that there are times in everyone's life when he/she will have a problem and will not know how to solve it. Adults often consult with counselors, friends, and others for help with their problems. This is called seeking technical assistance.

Have a discussion with the students about problems and about how to identify times when students need help. When a student recognizes that he/she needs help with a problem, he/she can seek assistance by going to the TAA. While in the TAA, the student should answer the following questions:

– What is my problem?
– What have I done to solve my problem?
– What kind of help do I need to solve my problem?

When a student enters the TAA, go over to him/her within two minutes and discuss the problem. Ask how he/she answered the three questions, and try to decide on the best solution (called an Assistance Plan). Discuss the following rules with the students and display them near the TAA:

– Only one student at a time in the TAA.

– Quietly read and think about the questions posted in the TAA.
– If a student is quiet and appropriately thinking about his/her problem, someone (teacher or teacher aide) will enter the TAA within two minutes to talk with the student. The student must be prepared to answer the three posted questions.
– After leaving the TAA, the student must attempt to use the Assistance Plan for a designated period of time prior to returning for additional assistance.

● The Help Center

This is similar to the Technical Assistance time-out, but is designed for elementary students. Designate an area of the room where help can be obtained. This area

should have a chair or desk where the student can sit and think. On the wall or taped to the desk is a poster that says:

– Why am I here?
– What have I done to solve my problem?
– What help do I need?

The same rules and procedures used in the Technical Assistance Time-Out are used in the Help Center.

Exclusion involves the removal of the student from the immediate environment supporting his/her behavior to an environment that does not support the behavior. Make sure you can see the student at all times. Some ways to use exclusion include:

● I'm a Clock Watcher

This technique is used with younger students or those with disabilities. Explain that there will be occasions when you will need to keep track of a certain amount of time, and you will direct a student to help you. Tell the student, "Go stand in front of the clock and tell me when two minutes have passed." For students who cannot tell time, you might say, "Go stand in front of the clock and tell me when the big red hand (the second hand) is exactly at the top." During these times, no one is to talk to the student.

● **Control Time-Out**

This is used when you want a student to control himself/herself. Explain that there will be occasions when you are aware that the student is losing control and needs to regain it. At these times, you will instruct the student to stand or sit and silently count to 20, or repeat a calming message. Practice until you and the students feel confident that the students can do it. Then, the time-out procedure can be used in any setting and at any time.

Seclusion is the time-out procedure most often considered in discussions or descriptions of time-out. It is the most restrictive form of time-out, and it should be used infrequently and with care, because it removes a student from the learning environment, from his/her peers, and from direct instruction

opportunities. This method should be used only after other interventions have failed. Unfortunately, this procedure may be the most abused type of time-out. It is often used without having tried other interventions, or it may be used as punishment rather than removal of positive reinforcement. It may also result in power struggles between teacher and student if not properly used. One of the most noted abuses of the procedure involves the failure of a teacher to monitor and evaluate the effectiveness of its use.

Systematic seclusion generally involves placing the student in a specifically designed room for a short period of time after a serious misbehavior, such as being out of control (refusing to stop an undesirable behavior when told to), aggression, property destruction, cursing, fighting, use of weapons, or real or potential threats to injure someone.

While in time-out, a student is expected to regain control over his/her voice, physical activity, emotional reactions, breathing, and thoughts. The student should also think about what he/she did to be sent to time-out, and what he/she will do differently the next time to avoid going in time-out.

At the end of the time-out period, instruct the student to come out of the time-out area and stand by the door. Describe the behavior that resulted in the student going to time-out. Assess his/her level of control by

asking, "Are you in control of your behavior now? Do you think you are ready to return to work?" If the student says 'no', discuss his/her reluctance to return. Try to see the student's point of view. If necessary, you could allow him/her to return to time-out. Repeat the exit procedure after a minute or two. (Limit these refusals to one or two.)

When the student is ready to return, tell him/her, "I want you to walk back to your desk (area) without saying or doing anything to anyone, and start work." If he/she needs to restore the environment, state what needs to be done (e.g., "I want you to pick up the things you knocked over and put them where they belong."). Do not allow other students to make teasing remarks. Give the student a short time (30 seconds to a minute) to begin work, then go over to the student, offer help with the work, and reinforce his/her self-control. For example, "I like the way you ignored those guys. I know it's not easy, but you are showing you know how to control yourself. I'm proud of you." If, before returning to the work area, the student engages in a behavior that would have sent him/her to time-out, then simply re-institute time-out. For example, "You swore. Return to time-out." Or, if the student is returning to the work area and intentionally knocks something over, say, "You knocked over the _____. Return to time-out."

Always document each time-out episode. Keep a written record of the student's name, the name of the person who directed the student to time-out, the date, the exact times the student entered and left time-out, a description of the behavior which resulted in time-out, and any difficulties entering or exiting time-out.

4 Think about how to apply time-out to your particular situation.

Decide which types of time-out to use with which behaviors. After you have considered all of the options, decide whether you feel that a time-out procedure is warranted. To help you decide which type of time-out to use and when to use it, consider the questions on Form 47. This planner should help focus you on your options so that you resort to the most intensive types of time-out only after you have tried other interventions first.

Follow some important guidelines when using time-out. There are some general guidelines that will help you successfully implement any type of time-out. You should always remain focused on the goal of time-out: for the student to gain control over his/her thoughts, emotions, and behavior. It is also important to use repeated trials; that is, instead of one or two very long

time-outs, you should use more frequent time-outs that are shorter in duration. Allowing students to repeat time-out gives them more opportunities to gain control and more practice with the mechanics of the process. Remember, your use of time-out should teach the student what he/she did to receive the time-out, what he/she should do

differently next time, how to gain control over his/her behavior, and how to problem-solve or seek assistance.

- Time-out should be short.
  - Two to five minutes, maximum
  - The younger the student, the shorter the time-out
  - The lower the student's cognitive functioning, the shorter the time-out
- Use time-out in all environments.
  - Include the lunchroom, playground, hallways, special area classes like art, music, and PE, etc.
  - If you can, teach parents to use the same procedures at home
- Teach students the hows and whys of time-out.
  - Be clear about the specific behaviors that result in time-out
  - Make sure students have lots of practice using time-out
  - Always post written rules in the time-out area
- Don't forget your other options.
  - Periodically review your reinforcement plan and continuum of consequences

- Reinforce the difficult students frequently and powerfully when their behavior is appropriate
- Intervene early in a pattern of behavior.
  - Observe carefully so you can recognize the student's typical chain of behavior
  - Stop the pattern of behavior before it's serious
  - Teach the student other responses
- Always monitor the student.
  - Absolutely never leave a student unsupervised in a time-out situation
  - Keep track of the number of time-outs and of their duration
  - When you're using many time-outs and they don't seem to be working, it's time for another problem-solving session
- FORGIVE!
  - When it's over, it's over; move on and start with a clean slate

guidelines for using time-out

5 Teach your students about time-out procedures.

Teach time-out just as you teach other lessons. It is important to teach the time-out procedures before you use them, because it is difficult to teach a new concept when a student is agitated, upset, angry, or hostile. Teach time-out procedures in the same way that you teach other academic or behavioral skills. Students should learn that a time-out is just like any other activity in the classroom. Taking a time-out should not be thought of as an opportunity to challenge authority, lose self-control, and escalate into dangerous behavior; rather, it is an opportunity to gain self-control before any of those things happen. Your teaching should be matter-of-fact and direct, and all students should practice the various forms of time-out. At a minimum, your teaching plan should include:

- A clear presentation that identifies and describes the behaviors for which time-out will be used

- A demonstration (modeling) of how to take a time-out

- Role play by students of the time-out procedures

- The rules for how to behave while in time-out

- A description and demonstration of the procedures you will use when a student leaves an exclusionary or seclusionary time-out

- A description of how you will document your use of time-out and how you will evaluate the procedure's effectiveness, especially exclusion or seclusion

Provide opportunities for practice.
When we learn a new skill, we must practice in order to gain proficiency. When we practice the skill correctly, we are more likely to perform correctly under normal circumstances. Just as you teach and provide practice for learning the rules in your classroom, you should also provide opportunities for students to practice time-out. Conducting frequent, teacher-monitored practices is one of the best ways of ensuring that your use of time-out will be effective. For students who are uncomfortable or unfamiliar with time-out, practice is even more important. When you plan your weekly or monthly schedule, make sure you include a block of time for time-out practice. It can be one short role play, a review of the rules, teacher modeling, and/or a question and answer session. Your students' ages, levels of intellectual functioning, behavioral competencies, and prior histories should all be considered when you decide on the practice schedule.

6 After time-out is over, move on.

Forgive and forget. Because time-out can be so stressful to both students and teachers, it is a good idea to take a break after completing the procedure. Take a moment, breathe deeply, and begin another activity. When time-out is over, it is over. Do not hold a grudge and do not continue to dwell on the misbehavior that caused all the trouble. Focus on reteaching desirable behaviors and on using your positive reinforcement techniques. Move on!

Forms
for
Chapter
9

form 46 What's the Pattern?

First, _____ does this:

_____

and/or says this:

_____

_____

and looks like this:

_____

_____

The next behavior is this:

_____

_____

and/or this:

_____

_____

Finally, he/she does this:

_____

_____

and/or this:

_____

_____

form 47 Time-Out Planning Sheet

Is it safe to ignore this behavior?	YES	NO
	Use Ignoring	Use Contingent Observation

If one of these responses works, stop here. If neither response works, consider the questions below.

Can I remove materials or change the environment?	YES	NO
	Use Removal of Materials Use Reduction of Environmental Conditions	Use Student-Controlled Time-Out

Is the student so disruptive as to interrupt teaching or learning?	YES	NO
	Use Exclusion	Use Removal of Materials Use Reduction of Environmental Conditions Use Student-Controlled Time-Out

Is the student able to control himself/herself in Exclusion?	YES	NO
	Use Exclusion	Use Seclusion

predict, avoid, and manage crises

Crises are sometimes unavoidable in school. Planning and preparation can help to decrease their frequency and minimize their intensity.

Crisis situations can be related to medical emergencies, natural disasters, and incidents of violent or threatening behavior. It is important to predict and control crises, so that their harmful effects are minimized. This chapter will focus mainly on behavioral crises, since these are the ones that school personnel are most likely to encounter, and they are often stressful or dangerous for students and teachers. However, many of the same principles will apply to all types of crises.

Chapter
10

What to Do and How to Do it

1 Increase your knowledge about crises.

Be clear on how to recognize a crisis.
A crisis can be defined as any occasion when a student's behavior requires immediate attention to protect the physical and/or psychological safety of that student, the teacher, or others. A student in crisis is out of control, unable to stop his or her behavior without assistance, and not responsive to instructions. His/her behavior is dangerous, or

potentially dangerous, and there is concern that someone may be harmed if the behavior continues. Some examples of behaviors that could instigate crisis situations are aggression toward others (kicking, biting, hitting, hair pulling, and throwing objects), ingestion of toxic substances, playing with potentially harmful objects, and starting fires. A detailed list of specific crisis behaviors can be lengthy and varied for students, especially students with emotional or behavioral problems. *The essential element in*

determining when behavior constitutes a crisis is the judgment that the behavior is dangerous and must be controlled immediately to protect the student or others from harm.

Acknowledge the importance of crisis training. When students exhibit aggressive, impulsive, or volatile behavior, it can quickly escalate into dangerous situations. These behavioral crises have the potential to cause physical and psychological damage, and can present a chronic threat to students, teachers, administrators, and parents. With the increasing number of students who have emotional and behavioral disorders, it is critical that teachers be knowledgeable and competent in crisis management. Unfortunately, while most schools have plans and procedures for dealing with specific emergencies like fires, tornadoes, or earthquakes, they lack plans and predetermined procedures for dealing with behavioral crises. The actions taken to manage a crisis will vary, depending on the stage of the crisis, the nature of the crisis, the age and physical size of the students, and many other variables. Overall, the best strategy for dealing with crises is to prevent their occurrence. Of course, prevention is not always possible, so it is a good idea to know how to manage crises when they occur.

2 Take a proactive approach to crisis management.

Remember to focus on prevention. The primary goal of crisis management is to minimize or prevent the occurrence of crises. The best type of crisis management is a well-designed and consistently implemented behavior management program that reduces the potential for crisis situations. Behavioral interventions should be implemented before the student loses control and engages in the crisis behavior. Attention should focus on identifying and

modifying those behaviors that immediately precede acts of aggression or other dangerous activities. Behavioral skills should be taught that inhibit, or are incompatible with, crisis behavior. You should also design your daily interactions with students to help prevent crises from occurring. Try the common-sense guidelines on this page to help decrease the frequency of crises.

Review the use of time-out. Many crises can be avoided if the time-out procedures discussed in the previous chapter are used consistently. If you find that crises are occurring frequently in your school, classroom, cafeteria, playground, etc., review the time-out options. It may be that you (and other adults) should be intervening earlier, before behaviors have escalated to a crisis

- An atmosphere of trust should be developed that lets everyone feel safe and confident that they will not be harmed. This is accomplished through clear statements concerning the rules about aggression.

- Consequences for rule infractions should be known ahead of time and should be consistently enforced by the teacher.

- Rule infractions should be dealt with unemotionally.

- Students should be allowed to save face and to keep their self-respect. Almost everyone gets defensive when caught doing something wrong. Talking to students alone, giving them time to think, and offering other options can all be "face-saving" responses.

- Teachers and other adults should not make threats. Power struggles should be avoided.

- Behavioral expectations should be clearly defined, and teachers should check to see if students understand them.

- Teachers should model calm, composed behavior for their students (especially in stressful situations).

- The "what" of behavior should be discussed, not the "why." Questions such as, "What are you doing?" are preferable to, "Why are you doing that?" "Why" questions often lead to confrontations and power struggles with oppositional students.

- Teachers should not argue with students. This causes conflict and power struggles, and provides ammunition for students to continue arguing. Remember, it is not always necessary to have the last word in order to be right.

- Every attempt should be made to intervene with the behavior before a conflict develops.

guidelines for avoiding crises

level. Review the descriptions and procedures in the chapter and use a form of time-out before you find yourself in a crisis.

Teach self-management skills. For older and more capable students, self-management training should be conducted. Many students, especially those with behavioral disorders and Attention Deficit Hyperactivity Disorder (ADHD), can learn to control their disruptive and impulsive behaviors. Training programs teach specific alternative coping responses for provocative situations. For example, *Aggression Replacement Training* (Goldstein and Glick, 1987) is an excellent curriculum for teaching social skills, anger control, and moral reasoning to students. Self-management and other aggression reduction procedures should be part of the Individualized Education Plan for every student with an emotional or behavioral disorder, and should be a priority for many regular education students as well. Students who master self-management skills will be less likely to engage in crisis behaviors. These skills were discussed in Chapter 8 and will be presented in more detail in Chapter 15; however, if you teach two or three steps that are easy for students to remember, they will begin to learn the process very quickly. Choose a simple strategy and make posters (a sample is shown on Form 48), use reminder cards, and practice the steps verbally until students start to use their skills.

3 Prepare yourself to handle crises.

Participate in crisis management training. There are three phases of effective crisis management: pre-crisis, crisis, and post-crisis. Teachers should be trained in all phases of crisis management. This type of training is especially important for teachers whose students have serious emotional or behavioral problems, because crises are inevitable with these students. For other teachers, also, crises are more common today than ever before. One of the most widely known crisis management training programs is the Crisis Prevention Institute. CPI is a "train the trainers" model. It is available in most parts of the country, and districts can select their own in-house trainers so that teachers can be trained on-site. *Interventions* by Sprick, Sprick, and Garrison (1993) also addresses serious behavior problems. This model includes information on how to clear a room and how to remove students when they are out of control. Most crisis

management training programs do include direct instruction in physical management techniques, but it is critical that you attempt no physical intervention without thorough training, parental information and consent, and administrative guidelines. Keep in mind that most students do not require physical management, and this type of response should be a last resort.

Develop your crisis management plan. Even in the best programs, crises will occur. Teachers must be prepared to manage these situations. Lack of planning can result in confusion, escalation of the crisis, and potential harm to the student and/or teacher. Recognizing this, teachers and parents should develop plans ahead of time for how they will deal with crises. Disciplined responses are difficult to make when one's safety is threatened. Therefore, potential crisis situations should be identified, crisis management plans developed, and interventions rehearsed prior to an actual crisis. Preventive planning is the key to successful crisis management. A crisis management plan should be developed for any student who has a history of aggressive, injurious acts or who engages in potentially dangerous behavior. The crisis management plan should be developed by a team of professionals, including the teacher, and should:

- Identify the crisis behavior

- Determine the individuals who will be called upon for assistance

- Articulate the specific steps to be followed during and after the crisis

Use Form 49 to write out your plan. The individual steps, and any physical management techniques, should be practiced until staff members are confident in their ability to intervene without risk of harm to the students or themselves. These procedures should be rehearsed as realistically as possible, so that when a crisis occurs, personnel can intervene quickly and effectively.

4 Teach the students what to do.

Focus on one or two critical behaviors. Many individuals haven't been taught to respond calmly and effectively during a crisis. You should not assume that your students know how to behave appropriately during a crisis situation. To avert panic, chaos, and/or injury during crises, teach your students what to do and how to do it. Following directions is essential for success in crisis situations. Students should be taught to respond to simple commands such as, "Go to (place)," so that when a crisis occurs, you will feel more confident giving instructions. To promote generalization, these responses should be taught and practiced at various times and in a variety of environments. Of

course, students' ages and levels of functioning will help determine how many behaviors to teach. Every student should be taught at least two basic behaviors to use during a crisis:

- Stop—no movement, talking, crying, yelling, or other disruptive responses

- Follow the teacher's (adult's) directions

Teach students to go for help. Depending on the students' cognitive ability, maturity, and ability to function independently, you may also want to teach them how to seek help during a crisis. If their adaptive behavior indicates that they are capable enough, they should be taught to identify people who can provide help and to know where these people can be found. Teach them to say "(Person's name) needs help," or simply "Help." Going to find help and bringing help to where it is needed should be rehearsed. Parents should be instructed

to teach these procedures at home, along with other skills such as dialing "911" on the telephone for help, and going to a neighbor for help.

5 Learn to predict crises.

Collect relevant information. Since the primary goal of crisis management is prevention, predicting when a crisis is likely to occur is essential. Teachers, especially those whose students have chronic behavior problems, often report that their students "blow up" without any warning. While blowups may sometimes occur, most crisis behaviors are preceded by cues and other signals. The problem is that the teacher either does not recognize the signals, or recognizes them but fails to take action soon enough to change the student's behavior.

One way to begin is to analyze the student's past behavioral history as well as his/her current behavior patterns. The best predictor of what will occur in the future is what has occurred in the past. Students with a history of aggressive, dangerous behaviors are more likely to engage in these behaviors than students who have no such history. A questionnaire such as the one on Form 50 may be useful in identifying the key factors in a student's behavioral history.

Analyze your information. Careful analysis of a student's history can provide useful information for determining if that student is likely to engage in crisis behaviors. Examine the information on your completed questionnaire. Identify the factors involved in previous crisis episodes. Determine whether there is a predictable pattern occurring before the crises. Look to the setting for clues, including factors like time, location, individuals involved, precursor behaviors, etc. Then try to predict future situations in which the student might lose control. If a clear pattern emerges, you can now design preventive interventions and prepare a more specific action plan to follow when the next crisis occurs. Once you think you can accurately predict a student's crises, share the information with other teachers, administrators, support personnel like bus drivers and instructional assistants, and the student's parent(s). While this planning may not eliminate crises, it will probably help you manage them more successfully and reduce their impact on everyone involved.

Sometimes, an audiotape can have a big effect on students. When a student is out of control or verbally abusive, calmly push the "record" button on a cassette recorder. You don't need to explain, threaten, or discuss. Just record, so that when you hold a conference with the student later, the student and his/her parent(s) can hear exactly what he/she sounds like.

- **Follow your crisis management plan.**
  - The interventions decided upon prior to the crisis should be put into action.
  - Send for help if you are not sure you can manage the situation safely. Remember, you will need at least two adults, so the other students are not left unattended.
- **Stay calm.**
  - Control your breathing and your outward responses.
  - Don't panic. Showing fear, anger, or other emotional responses will not help control the situation. When a teacher becomes upset, it usually causes the students to become upset, and the entire class may panic.
- **Give the student some space.**
  - Don't invade the student's "personal space."
  - If the student isn't physically attacking anyone, stand a safe distance away. A distance of eight feet is usually safe, yet sufficient for you to see and prepare for physical attacks. Commands and requests can be made without using a loud voice, and if you need to take physical action, you are close enough to move quickly.
- **Tell the student why he/she should stop the behavior.**
  - The student may need to be told why his/her behavior is unacceptable. Give a clear rationale for why the student should stop. Usually, the rationale is that the behavior is dangerous to the student or to others, but you can also refer to rules, social expectations, and other reasons that the student is aware of.
  - Try to relate personally ("Andre, it would help me a great deal if you would calm down."), to appeal to the student's values ("Sharon, do you think it's OK to hurt people?"), or to speak to his/her sense of self ("Roy, you're too smart to let this get out of hand. Let's talk it over.").
- **Use as little action as necessary.**
  - Before taking any physical action, tell the student to stop the behavior. Sometimes a loud "No!" will immobilize the student.
  - Give the student time to stop. Older students may calm down in a minute or two; younger students may need about five minutes.
  - Don't attempt a physical intervention if you are not confident that you can do what is required. Wait for help to come.
- **Don't counteraggress.**
  - Student aggression countered by teacher aggression will frequently cause an escalation in the student's behavior. The student may become even more angry and more dangerous.
  - If the student becomes aggressive, you should not strike back. Instead, if possible, move out of striking range and tell the student to stop.
- **Use physical management techniques only as a last resort and only if you are well-trained.**

guidelines to follow during a crisis

6 Know what to do during a crisis.

Follow some basic guidelines. Regardless of the type of crisis, it is important to bring the student's behavior under control. This is not easy to do when a student is engaging in dangerous behavior. However, listed on the previous page are some practices that will help.

7 After the crisis, work with the student.

Use a time-out procedure if necessary. After the student is under control and not physically dangerous, he/she may require a seclusionary time-out. The time-out should be long enough for the student to calm down and regain his/her composure. Usually, two to five minutes is sufficient. While in time-out, the student may rage and vent emotions by screaming, crying, or physically attacking the time-out room. If he/she becomes self-injurious, you or other staff must intervene. Comments should be minimal and should be used only to tell the student what is required. For example, "Frankie, no hitting! When you're quiet, you can return to class."

After the time-out, process with the student. After the student is quiet for two to five minutes, announce, "Time-out is over. We're going back to class." Before returning

to the classroom, state the reason the student was placed in time-out and have the student repeat it. For example, "Tom, you were put in time-out for hitting. Tom, why were you put in time-out?" If the student responds incorrectly, repeat the statement. If, after two or three trials, the student continues to respond incorrectly, state the rule clearly and ask if the student understands. For example, "When you hit, you will go to time-out. Do you understand?" If the student says "No," or doesn't respond, you should restate the reasons the student was placed in time-out and describe the expectations for the return to the classroom, including what he/she is to do after returning. The following dialogue may serve as an example: "Nina, you are to walk back to class. You will pick up the things you knocked over. If you knock things over again, you will return to time-out." Return the student to class and immediately engage him/her in ongoing class activities. Be attentive to desirable behavior and reinforce it frequently. If negative behavior occurs, deal with the student according to his/her management plan.

8 Review the incident.

Record all pertinent information. As soon as possible, record what happened during the crisis. Form 51 can be completed to guide you in your evaluation of the events. Significant aspects of the crisis episode should

be noted in detail. Copies should be made and distributed to the building administrator, parent(s), and any others designated to receive the report. The student's parent(s) should be informed of what happened. If necessary, schedule a meeting with the parent(s) to discuss the student's behavior and the nature of the crisis. File a written report if your school procedures call for it, and distribute it to the appropriate personnel.

Reteach. The post-crisis phase should focus on teaching all the students to identify their behaviors before, during, and after the crisis, especially if the student in the crisis was physically managed or was given a seclusionary time-out. At this point, it may be a good idea to review the class rules, consequences, and positive reinforcement system. That student should also be required to problem-solve and to generate alternative options for future behavior. There are two helpful forms (Forms 52 and 53) at the end of this chapter that will help students process what happened, why, and how they can behave differently the next time. Ask the student to fill in the information and discuss it with you.

Forms
for
Chapter
10

form 48 Stop, Think, Proceed

stop

Stop moving
Stay calm and start to think

think

Decide what the problem is
Think of at least two solutions
Figure out advantages and disadvantages for each solution

proceed

Choose your best alternative and go with it

form 49 Crisis Management Plan

Name: _____

Crisis Behavior: _____

_____

Persons to notify: _____

Actions to be taken: Who will do this:

Step 1: _____   _____

_____   _____

Step 2: _____   _____

_____   _____

Step 3: _____   _____

_____   _____

Step 4: _____   _____

_____   _____

Step 5: _____   _____

_____   _____

Step 6: _____   _____

_____   _____

form 50 Crisis History Questionnaire

Student:_____ Teacher:_____

1. What is the student's history relative to crises?

    ● Have there been past incidents of dangerous behavior? Yes ❑ No ❑

    ● Describe the nature of the behavior as specifically as possible: _____
    _____

    ● When did this behavior most recently occur? (List date & time) _____

    ● Is there a specific time of day when this behavior tends to occur? Yes ❑ No ❑ When?_____

    ● In what setting did the behavior last occur? _____

    ● Has this behavior occurred before in this setting? Yes ❑ No ❑ When?_____How frequently? _____

    ● Who was present in this setting? _____

    ● What events led to the behavior? _____
    _____

    ● What action did the adult(s) present take to deal with the crisis?_____
    _____

    ● How effective were the adult's actions? _____

    ● Is there any observable pattern to the behavior?_____
    _____

    ● Give any additional information that might account for the student's behavior: _____
    _____

(cont'd)

form 50 (cont'd)

2. What behaviors precede a crisis?

  ● Describe, in as much detail as possible, any behavioral signals that typically precede the student's crises. For example: Crying, anger signs, lack of responsiveness, self-stimulations, self-injurious behaviors, etc. _____

    _____

  ● Of the behaviors listed in the previous item, which ones are most likely to be followed by a crisis? _____

    _____

3. Describe the relevant behavior management strategies.

  ● What behavior management strategies have previously been used to prevent the student from escalating into a crisis? _____

    _____

  ● Which strategies were most effective? _____

  ● Which strategies were least effective and probably shouldn't be used again with this student? _____

    _____

  ● Is the student currently on any medication? ❑ Yes ❑ No If yes, what type? _____

  ● Does the medication cause any negative behavioral side effects? ❑ Yes ❑ No If yes, describe: _____

    _____

  ● When was the medication last prescribed? _____

  ● Student's last contact with physician: _____

  ● Are there any known conditions (e.g., recent deaths, separations, abuse, etc.) that could be causing the student's crisis?
    ❑ Yes ❑ No If yes, describe: _____

  ● Do peers influence the occurrence of the crisis? ❑ Yes ❑ No If yes, describe: _____

    _____

  ● Describe any other known conditions that could be helpful in predicting the student's crises: _____

    _____

form 5 1 Critical Incident Report

Student:_____ Today's date: _____

Person completing form:_____ Date/time of incident: _____

1. In objective terms, describe the incident, including the specific sequence of events, the location, and the persons involved. _____

_____

_____

_____

2. Who was present and witnessed the incident? _____

3. What happened before the incident? Describe in sequence. _____

_____

4. What behaviors (signals, cues, etc.) did the student demonstrate immediately prior to the crisis?_____

_____

5. What action was taken to prevent the incident?_____

_____

6. Describe the intervention(s) used._____

_____

7. Was anyone injured? List names and nature of injuries._____

_____

8. Who was notified?_____

9. Is there a crisis management plan for this student? If yes, was the plan followed? If no, why not? _____

_____

form 5 2 Behavior Improvement Form

Room Clear: ❏   Time-Out: ❏   Did you follow directions appropriately? ❏ Yes ❏ No

Name: _____ Date: _____

1. What was your behavior? _____

_____

2. What did you want? (Check at least one.)
❏ I wanted attention from others.
❏ I wanted to be in control of the situation.
❏ I wanted to challenge the teacher's authority.
❏ I wanted to avoid doing my work.
❏ I wanted to be sent home.
❏ I wanted to cause problems because I am miserable inside.
❏ I wanted to cause others problems because they don't like me.
❏ I wanted revenge.
❏ I wanted_____

3. Did you get what you wanted?   ❏ Yes ❏ No

Why?_____

_____

4. What could you do differently?_____

_____

5. Will you be able to do it appropriately?   ❏ Yes ❏ No   Student's Signature: _____

Reviewed by:_____

form 53 Problem Solving Form

Teacher Section

Student Name:_____ Date: _____

Reason for Referral to Problem Solving: _____

Student Section

1. Why were you sent to Problem Solving? _____

2. How were you feeling when you were sent for help? _____

   _____

3. What could you have done differently? _____

   _____

4. What could the adult involved have done differently? _____

   _____

5. How do you feel now? _____

   _____

6. What will you do differently next time? What is your immediate plan to improve your relationships with others? _____

   _____

7. Is there anyone else whom you would like to involve, either right now or the next time you are upset?_____

   _____

Student Signature:_____Staff Signature: _____

PART THREE

Effective Classroom Management and Instruction

put together a management system

Establishing a total management system for your class can result in a positive classroom environment that is respectful and encouraging.

In most schools today, there are many students who can benefit from a total management system. A class-wide or school-wide management system with a hierarchical approach can provide a clear structure for improving students' academic and social skills. Systems can also help you maintain a positive focus, so that you and your students have a good time together. Total management systems are effective with students, enjoyable for teachers, and easy to implement consistently.

What to Do and How to Do it

1 Consider what area you'd like to focus on.

Begin to think about your purpose.
Most management systems are designed for the purpose of improving students' behavior. The final system created should fit your individual needs and those of your students. Each individual management system will also have its own objectives, activities, criteria for student performance, and methods

for measuring progress. Some class-wide or school-wide management systems are very comprehensive; other systems are more loosely organized and involve only one component, usually positive reinforcement strategies. The first step in designing a total management system for a class, academic or grade-level team, or school is to decide on your overall purpose. Then you can begin to establish your more specific objectives.

"A straight path never leads anywhere except to the objective." Andre Gide

Determine the needs of your students.
Before beginning to design any management system, it is important to determine your students' needs. There are several ways to evaluate those needs:

● Discrepancy analysis—This is a simple matter of determining which skills you think your students need versus the skills your students have already mastered. There are formal and informal techniques for determining students' competencies, especially in social skills. These have been discussed in more detail in Chapter 5, and that chapter contains a checklist that you can use when you evaluate students' behavior.

- Check of social validity—Consider which skills will be most critical for students' success in life, including those skills necessary for job success and interpersonal relationships.

- Consideration of the group as a whole—Consider which skills are critical for a productive and successful group. Are there any skills that almost all of the students lack? Are there one or two skills whose absence is interfering with learning? After examining all of these issues, you can clarify your purpose and begin to decide on a few of your more specific goals. Some examples of areas you could focus on for comprehensive management systems are:

Improving listening skills, including:

- Passive listening (sitting still, looking at the teacher, quiet hands)
- Active listening (questioning, taking turns, rephrasing, making positive comments)

Problem-solving skills, including:

- Self-monitoring (describing feelings and actions, recording one's own behavior, measuring individual progress, self-evaluation
- Decision making (setting realistic goals, articulating choices, describing advantages and disadvantages, locating resources)

2 Clearly establish your target behaviors.

Objectively describe the skills you're going to teach. After you have decided on the specific skills you want to emphasize in your system, describe them objectively. This is important, because both you and your students must know what is expected. To describe skills in terms that can be observed and measured, you can use the simple format presented on Form 54. This structure will guide you in describing behaviors that

can be measured and evaluated objectively. It is also helpful if you put your target behaviors in a hierarchy or continuum, so that prerequisite skills are taught first. Keep in mind that while you probably consider some behaviors to be non-negotiable, you can be flexible about some less critical behaviors. Before you begin, go back to Form 19 in Chapter 5 and use it to help you identify specific behaviors. Then, decide (based on your discrepancy analysis, check of social validity, or whole group needs) where to begin.

Set realistic criteria. Keep in mind that most students in school haven't mastered all of the skills necessary for success. If they had, you probably wouldn't need to create a management system. Some students have behavior problems that disturb teachers, parents, peers, and even themselves. Therefore, it is not realistic to expect students to immediately demonstrate complete mastery of your system's targeted skills 100% of the time. While it is important to maintain high expectations for students, demanding absolute perfection is counterproductive. If you wait until all of your students demonstrate perfection before you reinforce them, everyone will be disappointed. Worse still, students may get the idea that any small steps they make aren't important or valued, and they may stop trying. We learn by mastering the basics first, then developing higher-level skills that build on them. Set realistic and obtainable criteria at first.

After students have met the initial criteria, be prepared to raise your expectations and to change the criteria accordingly. For example, many level systems increase the percentage of demonstrated mastery required: at Level 1, students may have to demonstrate target behaviors 80% of the time, but for Level 2 privileges, the requirement may be 90%. When you decide on your initial criteria for success, also decide when you would like to change your criteria. One commonly used guideline is to raise criteria after 10-15 school days of success at the lower level.

Tell your students what you want.

Being a student can become very confusing. When Roland's language arts teacher, Mr. Poole, talks about listening skills, he means that he wants students quiet and in their seats when he gives directions. When Roland goes to science, though, Ms. Crosby doesn't care if students are seated. When Ms. Crosby says, "Listen," she wants students to simply stop what they're doing and look at her face. If Roland is going to please both Mr. Poole and Ms. Crosby, he needs to learn what each of them wants. Again, use Form 19 in Chapter 5 to define target social skills; you can also use this tool to define cooperative learning skills. Using the T-chart, discuss with your students exactly what essential behaviors you want to see and hear. These behaviors will be the indicators for mastery of the target skill. It's also a good idea to allow students to contribute their ideas to the chart. They probably have good insight into the factors that contribute to everyone's success in the classroom. After you've finished the chart, make sure that everyone can describe the skills clearly and can recognize examples and non-examples when they see them.

3 Decide how you will evaluate behavior.

Choose a monitoring system. In Chapter 8, we showed several different ways that you can monitor the behavior of individual students. It is not always possible or practical to monitor the entire group's behavior in the same ways. You need to develop a system that is easy to administer, requires little bookkeeping, and can be clearly understood by everyone. Your monitoring system can easily be linked to your reinforcement system, since you will hopefully be using lots of positive reinforcement for good behavior. This section presents some simple ideas for monitoring a group.

Try implementing a banking system. Print some play money with your face, your name, or some other personal logo to identify it. Students can earn and spend the money according to your rules. Charge fees for things like desk rent, supplies, special events, etc. Pay students for things like demonstrating target behaviors, staying on-task, returning forms from home, etc. Use bonuses and fines for unique situations, and encourage life skills by designing checkbooks, ledgers, etc. You could add interest with an "in-class garage sale." Allow students to bring in their old toys, CDs, books, etc. and set up shop once per month. You can also collect donations or ask for PTA help. When it's time to spend the play money on positive reinforcers, consider using a "catalogue" that has pictures and/or descriptions of items that are "for sale" in the classroom. Using a catalogue is a great way to reinforce reading and math skills; it also cuts down on wasted time and on movement when students "go shopping." Students can simply fill out and hand in a completed order form.

We've created a sample banking system called "Bonus Bucks" to help start you out.

Looking at the suggestions here and at Forms 55-57 may help you visualize how a simple idea can be adapted to work for a whole class. "Bonus Bucks" is easy to use and fun for students. Follow these guidelines for using the system:

- Focus on the most important behaviors, prioritizing from least to most critical/problematic (e.g., following an adult's first request, remaining in work area, staying in seat, etc.).

- Identify behaviors that are absolutely not permitted, such as hitting others.

- Discuss with the class which positive reinforcers they value most, both at school and at home, if desired (e.g., going for a walk, reading the newspaper, earning computer time, buying CDs, going to the mall, etc.).

- Decide on what amounts will be earned for positive behaviors, and what fines will be assessed for problem behaviors.

- Decide on a schedule for spending—have some small items for during the day (e.g., soda at lunch) and some biggies for the end of the week and the month.

- Use notebooks to organize students' checkbooks, etc.

- Use a metal money box for storing the Bonus Bucks. Lock it and store it at school.

- Make sure that everyone is clear about the system and about how they will be evaluated. Then, *be consistent.*

Use a "fill-in system." Start with a funny or exciting picture that has lots of sections, spaces, or grids, such as a geometric design, a page of repeating shapes, a checkerboard pattern, etc., and enlarge it to poster size. Color or fill in one part at a time, whenever the whole class demonstrates the target behaviors. When the entire poster is complete, the class earns a special group reward. For a student who needs extra incentives, make him/her the "hero." When he/she demonstrates a skill you want, the class earns double credit.

Include something three-dimensional. Fill a jar or box with Ping-Pong® balls by adding one each time a target behavior occurs, or add to a paper chain of handprints or loops that will eventually stretch from one side of the room to the other. Or, you could raise a flag or balloon a little higher each time students meet criteria.

4 Now decide how to put it all together.

Go back and review. If you have not read the preceding chapters on rules, positive reinforcement, and consequences, you may wish to do so now. If you did read them, but have forgotten what you read, go back and review. If you have written clear rules, developed effective positive reinforcers, and designed a fair system of consequences, you can now put them together with your target behaviors to form a total management system. One way to accomplish this is to use an organizational form, which is especially effective if you have decided to use a level system. Form 58 will help you define what you expect as your students work their way up the hierarchy toward excellence in your system. Make sure that your behaviors are presented in a hierarchical order, with the most basic first, and higher-level skills later. It is also very important that your system not replace individual goals and objectives, especially for students with disabilities. It is neither legal nor advisable to design a comprehensive system that ignores individual needs.

Write down your system rules and procedures.
Again, put all of your other information together. Use Form 59 to guide you, and work through the items on the form. At a minimum, you will probably want to include:

- A name for your system

- The focus and general purpose of your system

- A general description

- A hierarchy of specific target behaviors

- Your expectations, including rules, criteria, reinforcers, and consequences (for individuals)

- An explanation of your monitoring system

- How students will progress through the system

- An explanation of how you will individualize for students with special needs

- A description of your evaluation plan (and timeline)

5 Assess your system.

Plan how you will collect information.
There are many ways to evaluate the effectiveness of interventions in school. Indicators can include data on attendance, discipline referrals, suspensions, incidents of aggression, time spent in general education versus special education, grades, test scores, etc. Much of this information is useful and relevant when evaluating your comprehensive management system. However, if you don't identify the information you want and collect it before, during, and after you implement your system, you may have problems: First, it may be difficult to retrieve or reconstruct past data. Second, if you don't keep up with your data collection on a daily or

weekly basis, you will have lots of work to do in the future, all at once. Finally, if you don't design a quick, easy system, you may not evaluate at all. Then you might never know how well your system really works. Before you begin your management system, decide what information to collect, figure out the easiest way to collect it, and assign specific individuals (including the teacher, teaching assistant, and students) to do specific tasks.

Before you begin, review your plan.
There are some critical questions to ask yourself once you are ready to implement your management system. These questions are common-sense considerations for class-wide or school-wide programs:

- Does your plan treat students with respect and dignity?

- Have you made plans to teach the target behaviors and rules?

- Is everyone clear about what the positive reinforcers and consequences are, and about how they will be used?

- Does the program have a hierarchy of skills and a clear sequence of consequences built into it?

- Have you made plans to evaluate? Do your plans include student input?

Forms
for
Chapter
11

form 54 Describing and Defining Target Behaviors

In order to achieve our overall purpose of:_____

The key behaviors we will focus on are these:

First, the students will: _____

Under these conditions: _____

Until they meet these criteria: _____

_____

The second key behavior is: _____

Under these conditions: _____

Until they meet these criteria: _____

_____

The third key behavior is:_____

Under these conditions: _____

Until they meet these criteria: _____

_____

The fourth key behavior is: _____

Under these conditions: _____

Until they meet these criteria: _____

_____

form 55 Bonus Bucks Management System

Bonus Bucks Can Be Earned for These Behaviors

At School	Amount	At Home (optional)	Amount
____	____	____	____
____	____	____	____
____	____	____	____
____	____	____	____

Bonus Bucks Will Be Collected as Fines for These Behaviors

Bonus Bucks Can Buy These Rewards

	Amount		Amount
____	____	____	____
____	____	____	____
____	____	____	____

form 56 Bonus Bucks

Copy these and cut them out to use with your class.

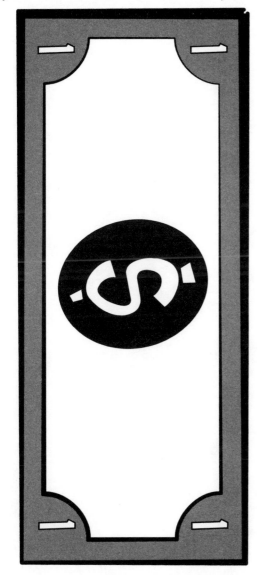
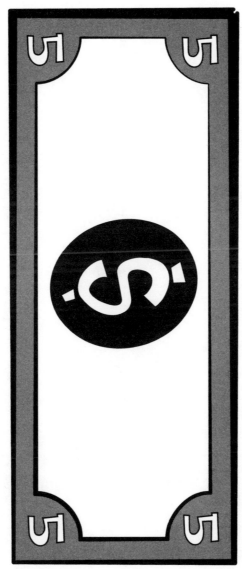
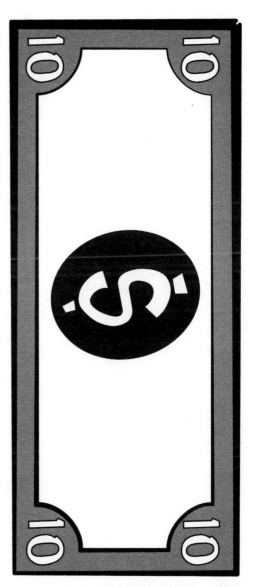

form 57 Bonus Bucks Additional Record-Keeping Forms (optional)

Copy these and cut them out to use with your class.

Student Checks

		_____ 19 _____		
Pay To The Order Of	_____	$ _____		
	_____	Dollars		
_____ School				
_____ , _____				
Town　　　　State				
Memo _____	_____			

Student Balance Book

		Record all charges or credits that affect your account.					BALANCE	
NUMBER	DATE	DESCRIPTION OF TRANSACTION	PAYMENT/DEBIT (-)	3 T	FEE (IF ANY) (-)	DEPOSIT/CREDIT (+)	$	
			$		$	$		

form 5 8 Planning Form

Level 1 Target Behaviors:

Criteria to determine mastery of target behavior(s): _____

_____

Reinforcers for displaying target behavior(s): _____

_____

Consequences for serious rule infractions: _____

Level 2 Target Behaviors:

Criteria to determine mastery of target behavior(s): _____

_____

Reinforcers for displaying target behavior(s): _____

_____

Consequences for serious rule infractions: _____

Level 3 Target Behaviors:

Criteria to determine mastery of target behavior(s): _____

_____

Reinforcers for displaying target behavior(s): _____

_____

Consequences for serious rule infractions: _____

form 59 A Description of Our Management System

We're calling the system: _____

Briefly, here's our focus and our general purpose: _____

_____

_____

_____

Here's how it's going to work: _____

_____

_____

_____

The target behaviors are (in hierarchical order):

_____   _____

_____   _____

_____   _____

Students will be expected to meet these criteria: If they do, they will earn these reinforcers:

_____   _____

_____   _____

_____   _____

_____   _____

(cont'd)

form 59 (cont'd)

If they don't, these will be the consequences:

_____   _____

_____   _____

_____   _____

_____   _____

We will monitor by (attach a sample or illustration if needed): _____

_____

Criteria for movement up or down (if using a level system):

_____   _____

_____   _____

_____   _____

_____   _____

We'll individualize by using these steps and/or tools: _____

_____

We'll evaluate on this schedule: _____

By using this information:_____

_____

individualize to meet students' needs

Students are individuals. Individualizing instruction to meet their unique needs is an integral part of good teaching.

With the increasing diversity in schools today, trying to teach the same thing the same way to everyone would not be a productive way to spend your time. Many students will require modifications and adaptations if they are going to succeed. You will probably spend less time reteaching and remediating later if you take the initiative to modify and adapt your instruction and your materials *before* you teach.

Chapter 12

What to Do and How to Do it

1 Look at individualization in a new perspective.

Consider that you've probably already begun. Modifying and adapting for more effective instruction is not new. Good teachers have always individualized to meet the needs of their students. Since public schools first opened their doors, there have been gifted and talented students who are extremely bright, lower-functioning students who require more reteaching and extra practice, students who have trouble concentrating, and students who are impulsive and hyperactive. The number of students with exceptional needs and abilities seems to be increasing, as does the severity of some students' problems, but many of the modifications that today's teachers make are the same things that teachers have always done. These individualization techniques are good teaching practices, and they will be necessary regardless of where or what you teach.

"There is no such thing as regular education any more." First-year teacher

Adopt a preventive outlook. If your instruction is appropriate and motivating, you can prevent many learning problems, and focusing on prevention is much more enjoyable than focusing on remediation. The preventive mind-set encourages us to think ahead, plan for success, and design creative alternatives to many ineffective teaching strategies. Teachers should be instructional leaders. As a teacher, you have control over many of the variables in the learning environment and can act as an agent of change in your classroom. So, educate yourself about your students' problems and needs. Continue to improve and refine your skills. Be a professional, demonstrating high ethical standards and a commitment to educating all students to their maximum potential. The changes that you make for the few students with learning problems will eventually benefit many students, as your teaching improves and you increase your repertoire of effective practices.

2 Begin with your instructional style.

Don't teach the same old thing the same old way. Few situations are more boring than being confined in a room where you can't move, listening to someone lecture to you all day long. Even if the content of the lecture is interesting, few teachers are exciting enough as presenters to use an all-lecture format and still keep students interested and motivated. Recent literature on learning styles has suggested what many teachers have known instinctively: different people learn different information in different ways. So, not only is it more enjoyable to vary instructional style, it is also a more effective way to teach. There

are several very effective formats of instruction which you can use, depending on the content area, the short-term goals, the ages and abilities of the students, and the length of the class instruction time available. Here are some alternatives to traditional, sometimes overused, instructional approaches:

- Instead of lecturing, use:

  - A panel discussion
  - A video or CD-ROM
  - A group discussion (with a small or large group)
  - An audio recording

- Set up situations in which students conduct their own inquiries. Let them:

  - State hypotheses
  - Observe actions and reactions
  - Test hypotheses
  - Interpret and synthesize information
  - Present conclusions
  - Classify and categorize information

- Stimulate active involvement with:

  - Experiments and simulations
  - Preparation and construction of exhibits
  - Games
  - Modeling and role play
  - Field trips in the community
  - Dramatizing

Change the way you give directions.

For many students, understanding and following oral and written directions is very difficult. This is especially true of students with attention problems or learning disabilities. Taking a slow, structured, clear approach to giving directions may increase the likelihood that students will pay attention, understand, and do what they have been asked. Using a slow, step-by-step method of giving directions may seem very time-consuming. However, a more deliberate approach may end up saving instructional time that would otherwise be devoted to questions, clarification, corrections, and reteaching. In Chapter 1, we presented a sequence of steps for giving directions. Now, here are some general guidelines for improving the way in which you give oral and written directions:

- For written directions:

  - Use copies that are clear and clean
  - Highlight, circle, or underline the key phrases in the directions

- Ask students to read the directions aloud
- Ask students to restate or paraphrase the directions
- Keep the directions short and simple
- Break the directions into several different steps
- Provide an example of a correct response for each type of question

● For oral directions:

- Make sure the students are looking at you ("Pencils down; eyes on me, please.")
- Provide the students with a cue for each step ("First", "next", "last")
- Put a written set of the directions on the overhead projector or the board, large enough for everyone to read
- After each separate direction, have the students repeat it
- Allow time for questions
- Model (demonstrate) if the task involves construction, movement, etc.

Start small. Teachers are always very busy people. When it is necessary to individualize instruction, start with the simplest, easiest modifications first. It is not always necessary to create a totally different assignment or lesson; sometimes, one or two minor adjustments to materials, instruction, or teaching style can make a big difference in student achievement. If the simple things don't

- Allow more time for a student to finish the assignment
- Shorten the assignment
- Allow a student to use a computer spell-checker
- Give "previews" (outlines with key points) of lectures, discussions, and media so students know what's important
- Try using overhead projectors to show key points while lecturing
- Call on a variety of students in random order so everyone stays involved
- Use a structured approach to giving directions (short, with cue words)
- Use peer partners for review
- Demonstrate and model with examples and non-examples
- Record lectures and read written material onto audiotapes
- Let students make flash cards and visual organizers, such as webs

some quick ideas for modifying

work, you can always move to a more labor-intensive, complicated approach later. This section lists some of the most practical modifications, strategies that most teachers can use without investing an inordinate amount of time and energy.

Provide students with advance organizers. Sometimes, teachers begin a lesson and very quickly realize that many of the students don't have any idea what they are talking about. Students may fail to make connections when teachers begin new topics without providing introductory material that students can relate to. Forms 60-62 are three tools that may help students focus on new material that is presented in lecture or written form. Form 60, a preview for students

to use, should help them find important information when they read or hear it. Form 61 is a box outline. The boxes will help students who have trouble with visual integration and organization, and the cue words should improve comprehension. Form 62 is a webbing structure used to help generate and organize vocabulary, classify information, and link related concepts. All three of these forms should help students by preparing them for an assignment. The forms can also help keep the students focused, so they remember the assignment's purpose as they complete the work.

3 Help your students appreciate their individuality.

Put them on the path toward self-reliance. If students rely on teacher assistance too much, they become dependent and helpless. Many students, especially those who have been in special education settings for a long time, are passive learners: They approach each task as though it were a totally unique, novel situation. This approach is not an efficient way to learn. If students fail to learn effective learning strategies, they may not make the connections necessary to absorb, analyze, and synthesize information quickly and accurately. Every task will be like starting over, even if they have already encountered similar information. They will also expect you, the teacher, to be at their sides helping them

every step of the way, something most teachers have neither the time nor the inclination to do. Students must grasp the hows and whys of learning if they are to successfully apply prior knowledge to new situations. The skills which help us learn to learn are called "meta-cognitive skills." They include study skills, memorization strategies, comprehension cues, test-taking skills, etc. These are described more completely in a following section.

Give them opportunities to work independently. Individualization does not necessarily mean that students all sit alone at their desks working on worksheets. However, it is helpful to allow students the space to pursue independent projects from time to time. There are effective ways to provide independent work that are enjoyable and stimulating for students. One of the best strategies is the use of individual learning projects, often in conjunction with contracts. One suggestion is to allow students to become "Classroom Experts." Students pursue an interest independently, then report back to the class on the results of their work. Form 63 is an excellent tool that allows teachers to structure students' learning and helps students keep track of their progress.

"Fair does not mean same."

Lynne Lewis, educator

4 Teach your students the basic skills they need.

Focus on the most important skills. There are some very basic skills that students will use in many educational situations, regardless of the content area. In helping your students become good learners, it is important to emphasize such critical competencies as:

- Effective listening
- Managing time wisely
- Organizing materials
- Planning and scheduling to meet deadlines
- Conducting research and writing projects
- Finding and using reference materials

Many students today come to school without having mastered these school survival skills. Unfortunately, many students also leave school still lacking them. If you find that your students have not mastered these and other important prerequisites for school success, stop and teach them, because it is unlikely that your students will pick them up naturally. After you provide direct instruction, remember to provide opportunities for practice, in many different subjects and content areas. A very good resource to help you in planning study skills instruction is John Seaman's book *Teaching Kids to Learn: An Integrated Study Skills Curriculum for Grades 5-7*. It is available from Sopris West.

Teach them an easy note-taking strategy. As students progress in school, it becomes more and more important for them to learn to take notes, both from written and from spoken material. While teachers often expect students to know some note-taking strategies, they usually don't take the time to teach those skills. One of the most helpful note-taking and studying strategies is an old standby, Three-Column Note Taking. This technique is simple and easy. Using a sheet of regular notebook paper (a sample is also shown on Form 64), students fold it lengthwise into three sections. On the left side of the page, students write key concepts in a word or two. The center section is used to record important subpoints or supporting details relating to each key concept. The far right column is used to write an elaboration on each key concept in the form of a short phrase. When studying, students can refold the paper on the fold lines so that their key concepts are on the outside. They read each key point and then try to recall the important supporting data. To check themselves, they can turn to the last column of their notes. This technique works well with almost any content area, and can even be taught to very young students.

Teach them to find answers in written material. Lots of students read and study without learning as much as they would like. If your students don't know how to determine which information is the most important and where the answers to questions are in a large body of text, teach them. There are several well-known strategies for teaching students how to read, listen, and study efficiently. It's important that your students learn one that works for them. Depending on a student's age, abilities, and prior academic experiences, you may want to help them develop either some very basic techniques or some higher-level, more complicated approaches. Here, we present a relatively simple strategy for finding answers in written material. Using this example as a starting point, you can help your students design personal strategies that work for them. You may need to design simple mnemonics to help them remember their strategies, or draw a symbol that reminds students when they can use their techniques. Begin by teaching these steps:

Step 1   READ the question.

Step 2   CIRCLE the key word in the question.

Step 3   READ the headings in the written material.

Step 4   SKIM through the material to find the key word you circled.

Step 5   READ the paragraph containing the key word.

Step 6   ASK yourself: Does this answer the question?

Teach them how to take tests, especially your tests. Many students do well on classwork and homework, but can't seem to excel on tests. Because the present structure of education relies heavily on tests as a measure of academic achievement, many students end up frustrated and confused. How can they know the information so well, yet do so poorly on the tests? Why are they able to demonstrate verbally what they know, but not able to produce on an exam? Almost all of us have experienced situations in which we knew the information but couldn't answer the questions. We think, "Why couldn't I think of that at the moment?" or, "I knew it so well. I just froze and couldn't remember anything." Unfortunately, some students experience these situations regularly. For them, underachievement on tests is more the rule than the exception. Familiarizing your students with your style and format of tests, providing practice tests, and teaching students some of the test-taking skills mentioned on the following page should improve their performance.

- How to study for tests, including highlighting, using note cards, rewriting, outlining, etc.
- How to deal with test anxiety. Teaching students some simple, unobtrusive relaxation techniques may improve their performance significantly.
- How to read directions, and how to decipher what the directions really mean.
- How to follow directions. This should be practiced, first with simple directions, then more complicated ones.
- How to think through what is being asked. This includes picking out the key words in the question.
- How to deal with specific test formats like true/false, multiple choice, and short answer.
- How to proofread and self-check.

test-taking skills to teach your students

5 Adopt an experimental mode of operation.

If at first you don't succeed ... The end of the phrase is, of course "... try, try again." Teachers often feel pressure to find the one correct answer to every question and the one perfect solution to every problem, but the complicated problems kids bring to school today are usually not solved by one pat response. We suggest that if you have been looking for the one approach that works with all students, you should abandon this pursuit. Adopt an experimental mode of teaching. Look at your students and develop a theory about what you think will work. Implement your strategy, evaluate its success, congratulate yourself if it works, and try another strategy if it doesn't. Modifying and adapting instruction and materials is not as difficult as it may seem. Small changes can make a world of difference in how hard students try and how well they eventually do in your classroom. It's OK if your first approach doesn't work. Just hang in there and try your next idea. Sooner or later, something you try will have a positive impact on your challenging student.

Forms
for
Chapter

12

form 60 Information Preview

Present this form to students before they begin to read a passage. Let them fill it in as they progress. This is especially useful in content areas like social studies and science.

Student:_____ Date: _____

Title:_____

Topic:_____

When is this all happening?_____

Where is the action? _____

Who are the important people? _____

What is happening (the problem, conflict, or key situation)? _____

_____

_____

_____

Why is this happening? Why are things the way they are? _____

_____

_____

_____

How is the situation solved or resolved? What happens?_____

_____

_____

_____

form 61 Sample Box Outline

When students are reading, but having problems with comprehension, try this box outline. Read over the key words first with students, then let them fill in the correct information for each box.

Name: _____ Date: _____

Setting (When and Where):
Important Characters:
Problem/Conflict:
Goal:
Actions Taken:
Outcome:

form 62 Webbing

Name: _____ Date: _____

fur

fast   predator

lion

eats meat   animal

wild   four legs

hunts at night

hyena

travels in
a pack

form **63** I'm the Classroom Expert

Name: _____ Date: _____

The Subject I Wanted to Study or Research: _____

_____

What I Wanted to Learn About my Subject: _____

_____

_____

The Sources I Used During my Research: _____

_____

_____

The Most Interesting Things I Found: _____

_____

_____

The Problems I Had: _____

How I Would Like to Present my Research to the Class: _____

_____

_____

Date I Will Make my Presentation: _____

form 64 Three-Column Note Taking

Students can organize their notes for later study by using this form. On the left, students should write the concepts being studied. In the center column, they can record important subpoints and details. The far right column is for short phrases that elaborate on the key concepts.

Key Concept	Details/Supporting Data	Notes

use cooperative learning structures

CORNER PIECE

Cooperative instructional arrangements allow students to learn both social and academic skills in an active, enjoyable format.

Many types of instruction are appropriate in school. In addition to traditional individualistic or competitive arrangements, you may want to consider cooperative learning. Cooperative learning situations have several benefits: They often include active, "hands-on" learning that students enjoy; they give students practice using social skills; and they facilitate higher-order thinking.

Chapter 13

What to Do and How to Do it

1 Become familiar with the concept of cooperative learning.

Define what cooperative learning is (and what it isn't). Cooperation is a common effort aimed at achieving a common goal. Cooperative learning involves more than just putting students together to complete identical, but individual, assignments; it is a small-group instructional design in which students work together to maximize their own and others' learning. Students share materials, ideas, and efforts in an attempt to reach a group objective. Much of our current instruction in school does not involve cooperation. Instead, we traditionally use direct teaching methods aimed at a whole class, then we evaluate learning with individual assignments, tests, and quizzes. Also, students currently spend much of their school time listening instead of doing.

Think about why you should use cooperative learning. You can use cooperative structures in your class not only to teach academics, but also to teach important life skills and social skills. Before you begin to use cooperative learning, think about your purposes. Cooperative learning, especially when used with diverse groups of students, can focus students on skills that are essential for success in relationships, families, and employment. Your personal commitment to developing students' real life skills can enhance their chances for success in all aspects of their lives.

"What do we live for if it is not to make life less difficult for each other?"

George Eliot

2 Focus on social behaviors.

Identify the social skills you would like students to use. Chapter 5 offered some ideas for identifying and describing specific social skills. Cooperative learning situations provide wonderful opportunities for learning and practicing these skills. When you plan cooperative activities, focus on social skills that fit the academic task and objective. For example, with preschool students, assigning roles like listener and talker can work well in a language arts activity that emphasizes active listening, turn taking, and cooperation. Older students who have mastered the social skills of listening and turn taking may still need practice, so you can create roles like encourager, reader, and writer. High-level, more complex social skills like negotiating, decision making, and problem solving must be clearly defined for students so that everyone is clear about expectations and about criteria for evaluation.

Be prepared to teach prerequisite skills. Especially for students who have little experience working in groups, or who have demonstrated poor social skills, mastering some basic cooperative skills is a prerequisite for

success in a group instruction atmosphere. Before you can use cooperative learning in your classroom, it may be necessary to teach basic cooperation skills. Fortunately, cooperative learning not only requires these prosocial skills, but can also be used as a vehicle for teaching them. These skills can be taught to very young children as well as to older students. It is also essential that you encourage positive peer support among students, because cooperative learning requires students to help each other complete the assigned tasks and, perhaps more important, to maintain their group as an effective, functional unit.

Decide which behaviors are most important for group functioning. Before beginning cooperative learning activities, it is important to set some standards for group

behavior. Here, we list some of the skills that are basic for successful group interactions. If your students haven't mastered these skills, make sure you use the cooperative learning situations to teach them.

3 Begin to establish standards for behavior.

Develop some basic rules for behavior within the groups. Decide on three to five behaviors from the list in the box that you believe are most critical for group functioning. After you have narrowed your list, work with your students to set some basic rules for how group members should behave. Explain to your students that in order for their groups to be successful, each student must work as part of a team. Shift the focus

- Staying with the group (close physical proximity)
- Active listening
- Using people's names
- Quiet voices
- Taking turns
- Asking questions
- Sharing materials
- Staying on-task
- Complimenting each other
- Accepting criticism, praise, or suggestions
- Offering to help
- Encouraging others
- Paraphrasing or restating others' ideas
- Summarizing
- Working together to evaluate your group's performance

basic skills for effective groups

from individual performance to the overall performance of the group. When developing rules, ask questions like: "What behaviors will help our group the most?"; "How can we encourage everyone in the group to do his/her best?"; and "How can we help each other reach our goal?" If you have already written and taught class rules, this may be just a review. However, keep in mind that group interactions sometimes require higher-level social skills than typical classroom situations do.

Take care to manage class behavior. Social skills can and should be emphasized within the groups, but class standards for behavior are also important, in order to keep things running smoothly during cooperative learning activities. Measures that govern the behavior of the class as a whole are essential to prevent excessive movement, noise, and off-task behavior. Try these suggestions for maintaining control when you have a room full of cooperative groups:

- Keep the noise down—Teach your students a signal that you will use when they become too noisy, such as:

  - A "shh" finger to lips sign
  - Two fingers up (the old peace sign)
  - Flashing classroom lights off and on
  - Moveable green, orange, and red signs or a "real" traffic light

- Manage participation—When you have some students who dominate and others who never get a turn, try these:

  - "Talk tokens" (each student receives the same number of tokens, and must use one each time he/she talks)
  - Using numbers within the groups to assign tasks ("All of the Number 1s do this"); this way students don't select tasks for themselves
  - Assigning one student in each group the job of making sure everyone gets a turn

- Build team identity and loyalty—Use these ideas before assigning academic tasks:

  - Starting with activities designed to build trust and share information

  - Using a "Round Table": one piece of paper, one pencil; the group works together to generate solutions, examples, or ideas like listing as many countries in the world or five-letter words as they can think of
  - Letting students choose names, logos, banners, cheers, etc. for their teams

- Keep students with their groups—Keeping movement to a minimum can prevent other behavior problems. Try these ideas for controlling movement:

  - Assigning one student per group to be materials manager so that fewer people are moving around the room
  - Reinforcing students for behaviors like staying with the group
  - Assigning one student in each group to be movement monitor

4 Begin your instructional planning.

Focus on the important elements of cooperative learning. There are three important guidelines for using cooperative strategies. First, you should structure cooperative learning tasks so that students are interdependent, that is, they need each other to complete the tasks successfully. You can structure interdependence in several different ways, which will be discussed in a following section. Second, you should require individual accountability as well as interdependence. This means that although the group works together to achieve a goal, students are still responsible for individual mastery of objectives. You need to evaluate both group and individual performance. Finally, for cooperative learning to be successful, students must interact directly with each other and must demonstrate positive social skills.

Decide on your group size. The size of the groups in cooperative learning situations depends on many factors, including the ages of your students, the social skill proficiency of the class, the nature of the assigned task, the length of time required to complete the task, etc. If your students haven't had a lot of experience working in cooperative groups, if they are very young, or if they lack some basic interaction skills, you might want to begin by using groups of two. A system of partners, buddies, or pairs

allows students to get used to working with another person, without the pressure of a large, diverse group. This box presents some ideas for two-student cooperative arrangements that will allow for easy, quick activities. After students have worked successfully in pairs, they are ready to begin to participate in groups that have three or more members.

- **Study Buddies**—One student reads while the other follows along and asks questions, then they switch roles
- **Partners**—One partner repeats the teacher's directions; the other asks questions and clarifies; before asking the teacher for help, they ask each other
- **Reading Pairs**—Two students read the same material; each writes answers to the comprehension questions, then they compare and produce their one best response for each question
- **Math Pairs**—Each student works the problems independently; they check each other's work, compare, and decide on the correct answers
- **Radio Readers**—Two students read in unison orally; this allows them to build their fluency and rhythm, as well as to model accurate reading for each other
- **Spell Checkers**—Pairs of students check each other's written work for correct spelling
- **Peer Editors**—Students edit each other's written work for punctuation, grammar, usage, and organization, using a different color pen than the teacher uses; students sign each other's papers after completing their editing (a more involved version is "Writing Response Partners," explained in a following box)
- **Lab Partners**—In the science lab, students work together to complete the project, handing in one completed assignment with both students' names on it

cooperative learning with pairs

Decide how to combine students into groups. The responsibility for structuring the learning environment rests with the teacher. Usually, you should be the one to make decisions about which students are in which groups, and for how long. Letting students select their own groups often results in consistent, predictable groups with the same students working together most of the time. Variety in group composition allows students to get to know everyone in the class, to learn to interact effectively with many different people, and to practice their interaction skills in a wide range of circumstances, some of which may be very challenging. This does not mean that student-selected groups are not desirable or useful, only that they may not always be appropriate. Here are some quick and easy ways to assign students to groups. Some are random, and some very structured. Keep in mind that the goal is to help students learn to work with all different kinds of people. In cooperative learning, diversity is a great tool for teaching social skills. Vary group membership so that there is a mix of genders, racial/ethnic groups, and ability levels.

Plan your cooperative activities. As with any other methodology, it is important to educate yourself about using cooperative learning. Locate as many resources as possible when you begin to use cooperative strategies. In the resource list, you will find information about materials that can help guide you as you structure cooperation within your classroom. They are excellent sources of practical, helpful information and are easy to read and understand.

Putting all of this information together into effective, motivating, interesting lessons

- **Stratified Random**—Use this for short units of instruction. Rank students from highest to lowest based on pretest of specific skills, past six weeks' grades, etc. In assigning students to groups, pick the highest, the lowest, and one or two from the middle. Repeat until all students are assigned.

- **Numbering**—Students count off by the number of groups. For example, to form six groups, students count off "one" through "six." Each student finds others with the same number, and they form a group.

- **Categories**—Decide how many groups you'd like, and select that number of categories. Write the name of each category (e.g., Rivers) on a sign, poster, etc. Write the names of category members (e.g., Mississippi, Amazon, Nile, Rhine) on note cards, and distribute the cards at random to students. Students form groups with others in the same category.

- **Eliminate the Isolates**—Have students list three peers they would like to work with. Identify isolates not chosen by anyone, or chosen by few others, and pair these students with socially skilled and supportive peers.

- **Math Method**—Each student solves a different math problem, then finds peers whose problems had the same answer (e.g., 3+3=__, 7-1=__, and 2x3=__).

- **States and Capitals**—Divide the number of students by two, and choose a geographic region of the country. Write the names of states on one set of cards, and the names of their capital cities on another set of cards. Distribute the cards randomly and let students find their partners.

- **Lineup**—Have students line up in order by some variable (birth dates from January 1 to December 31; alphabetical order, etc.). Fold the line in half by asking the first person to walk to the end of the line and stand opposite the last person. The rest of the line follows until each student is standing directly opposite someone else. Students can work as partners with whomever they're facing, or you can combine the pairs into groups of four.

- **Literary Characters**—Give each student a card with the name of a character from a selection of literature that everyone has read. Students work with others who are from the same play, story, or poem.

- **Alphabet Partners**—Take the student whose name is first on your alphabetical class list and pair him/her with the student whose name is last. Then pair the second student with the second from the last, etc.

assigning students to cooperative groups

- **Limit Materials**—When students must share materials to complete a task, working together is almost unavoidable. Distributing limited reference materials, only one answer sheet, or only one set of supplies are good ways to force students to share.

- **Require One Product**—Even if students in a group are sitting together and working on the same task, as long as each student produces his/her own product, group members will likely work in a parallel fashion, not interdependently. On the other hand, if you structure assignments so that the group must complete one product jointly, they will have to cooperate.

- **Jigsaw the Tasks**—Assign each student one part of a task, then require him/her to share the material with others in the group. For example, Marla may be required to read one section of text, while Tony reads another, and Marian the third part. When they get together, each student summarizes and reports on his/her material, and they all complete a related task.

- **Focus Trios**—Before a film, lecture, or reading assignment, students discuss and write down what they already know about the subject. They compile a list of questions on the material. After the presentation, the group answers their own questions and writes a report with the new information they have learned.

- **Drill Partners**—Pairs of students drill each other on spelling, vocabulary, math facts, etc. If both partners score above a certain grade on a quiz, they both earn bonus points.

- **Writing Response Partners**—In this structure, students read and respond to each other's papers three times. First, they mark what they like with a star and put a question mark beside what they do not understand or think is weak. Next, they mark mistakes in grammar, usage, punctuation, and spelling, and discuss them with their partners. Finally, they proofread each other's final drafts.

- **Group Report**—Students research a topic together. Each person is required to check a different source and to produce five note cards of information. Then they compile their information and produce one report.

- **Reading Groups**—In groups of three, students read material together and answer questions. Each is assigned a role: reader, checker (makes sure each person has an answer), or recorder. The group must come up with three possible answers to each question, then circle their favorite. When they are finished, all three must sign the group's paper to indicate consensus.

fostering interdependence in groups

requires planning. Use Form 65 to help you create cooperative learning activities that work for your students and for you.

5 Structure the groups.

Assign students to specific roles. Assigning specific roles in cooperative groups has the effect of requiring each student to practice a specific social skill. For example, if you assign Mike the role of encourager, he must focus on making positive statements, offering assistance, and/or sharing ideas. When you assign students to roles within their cooperative groups, consider both the social behaviors necessary to keep the group functioning effectively (the *process* roles) and the tasks required to complete the academic assignment (*product* roles). Form 66 is a checklist that should assist you in planning role assignments. It is important to assign roles that are appropriate for your students' abilities, the size of your groups, and the assigned tasks. Change students' roles frequently, so that all students have an opportunity to practice a variety of skills. One way of promoting better social behavior is to assign students to perform behaviors that they have not demonstrated consistently. For example, assign the negative student the role of complimenter or let the whiner have the role of encourager.

Structure the assignment for interdependence. Many academic tasks (especially those involving higher-order cognitive skills) that are typically designated as individual assignments can easily be adapted for group work. Many of these assignments would be more meaningful if they were completed by a group instead of by individual students. However, giving an assignment to a group for completion does not automatically guarantee that the students will work together effectively. Nor does group work always result in shared responsibility. In fact, one common complaint from students (and their parents) is that many group assignments result in inequitable labor, with some students doing most of the work and other students very little. It is the teacher's job to structure cooperative situations so that students must function interdependently to complete a task; try some of the suggestions listed on the previous page.

6 Decide how you will evaluate students' learning.

Establish your criteria for the group's performance. In cooperative learning situations just as in individual learning, it is important to decide on minimum standards that indicate a level of acceptable performance. These criteria should be clearly explained to the students, and can be used as a basis for assigning grades or expressing

approval. For example, you may evaluate a written report by using standard guidelines for writing, evaluate a product by determining the presence or absence of specific components, or evaluate completed problems on the basis of a percentage correct. When grading, you may wish to give the same grade to all students in a group, to give two grades to each student (one individual and one for the group), to grade the individual parts of the project and calculate an average to give to each student, or to use "satisfactory/unsatisfactory" for the group and give individual grades on social skills. If group grades are going to be assigned, the policy for grading should be clearly explained in writing to both students and parents. You should also decide ahead of time how to handle those students who consistently refuse to work with their groups or who fail to complete their parts of the group assignments.

Plan to evaluate individual performance. Even though students work in cooperative groups, individual mastery of skills is still very important. Plans should be made to evaluate each student's mastery of the skills that were required in the group activity. This can be done in many ways, some

informal and some formal. Following are some good ways to evaluate individual performance after a cooperative activity:

- Random Oral Checks

  After the groups have completed their activities, ask each group to assign numbers to its members. Ask all of the Number 1s to stand and be ready to answer the first question. The Number 2s can answer the next question, and so on. Students can write a response on the board, answer in unison, or be called on in random order.

- Spinner and Arrow

  After assigning roles to group members, arrange the role names on a circular spinner. Spin the arrow for each group; the student whose role is indicated answers a question for that group.

- Popping

  After you ask a question, one student at a time stands ("pops up") to answer for the group. Each student must pop up with an answer at least once.

- Traditional Tests, Quizzes, and Assignments

  Even though learning activities are designed for groups, teachers are not limited to whole group evaluation. In addition to your group evaluation, keep using individual assessments to measure individual learning.

- Team Jeopardy!®

One of the most enjoyable strategies for measuring student learning is to play a school version of the popular Jeopardy!® game show. Have students write some questions that test knowledge of a lesson or a unit of instruction. Arrange the questions by categories, and from least to most difficult, and write them on a poster or board. Then, randomly select one member from each team. These students will compete by answering questions on the content of the assignment.

Help students review their own progress. After a cooperative learning activity, students should not only evaluate their academic progress, but also look at how well their group functioned. This means that each student's performance in his/her role should be examined. When evaluating, students can be encouraged to ask themselves questions like:

- "How did we function as a group?"

- "Did each of us contribute to the group's success?"

- "What goals do we have for the next time we work together?"

- "What can we do to improve our group's performance?"

Students can refer to the group rules and the specific target behaviors you identified to help determine whether they were successful. Students can also do short self-evaluations that include ratings (like those on Form 32 in Chapter 6), yes/no questions, or open-ended discussions guided by the teacher.

Plan for generalization. There are many ways for you to evaluate students' cooperative group skills; observation, videotaping, checksheets, or rating scales like the *Scales for Predicting Successful Inclusion* (Gilliam & McConnell, 1996) can all be used. After your evaluation of students' progress in their cooperative groups, you can provide suggestions and plan activities that will generalize students' use of prosocial skills to other settings. Encouraging students to use their cooperative skills in other classes, the cafeteria, on the bus, at home, at their jobs, and with their friends outside of school will make the cooperative lessons more relevant. Remember, working as an effective member of a group is a lifelong skill and will help students succeed in relationships and in the world of work.

Forms
for
Chapter
13

form 65 Cooperative Learning Lesson Plan

Content area(s): _____

Academic objective(s): _____

_____

_____

Social skill(s) to be addressed: _____

_____

_____

What We Want to See:

_____

_____

_____

Group size: _____

Composition of groups (how members will be selected): _____

_____

Room arrangement:_____

Materials needed: _____

_____

Roles needed within each group (titles and descriptions):

_____   _____

_____   _____

What We Want to Hear:

_____

_____

_____

(cont'd)

form 65 (cont'd)

Lesson Content

Academic task: _____

Measures for ensuring interdependence: _____

Measures for ensuring individual accountability: _____

Monitoring

Criteria for success on academic objective:_____

_____

Observation method and procedures (Attach sample of observation form if applicable): _____

_____

Plans for giving feedback: _____

_____

Strategies and Formats for Evaluation

Task achievement:_____

Individual use of social skills:_____

Overall group functioning: _____

Troubleshooting

Method for dealing with the passively uninvolved student: _____

_____

Method for dealing with the student who takes over/dominates:_____

_____

form 66 Roles for Students: Which Ones Fit?

Listed are some possible roles that you could assign to group members. In planning your group activity, select those roles that fit your students' social needs, or are necessary to complete the assignment. Use the titles that fit your students' interests, ages, and abilities. Many of the roles listed here have similar meanings. Pick the ones necessary to get the job done and be sure to explain the responsibilities to the students.

Process Roles

_____ Encourager
_____ Praise giver
_____ Rule reminder
_____ Consensus/agreement checker
_____ Greeter
_____ Turn assigner
_____ Cheerleader
_____ Chooser
_____ Thanker
_____ Leader
_____ Coach
_____ Listener
_____ Negotiator
_____ Referee
_____ Smiler
_____ Questioner

Product Roles

_____ Spell checker
_____ Note taker
_____ Reporter
_____ Timekeeper
_____ Paster
_____ Materials manager
_____ Traffic cop
_____ Reader
_____ Artist
_____ Explainer
_____ Cutter
_____ Finder
_____ Seeker
_____ Counter
_____ Checker

motivate students to learn

Motivating students to learn is an important step in successful teaching.

It would be wonderful if all students were highly motivated and eager to learn. However, students are sometimes not intrinsically motivated. They may find school boring, learning difficult, and academic content uninteresting and irrelevant. While it is not possible to motivate all of your students all of the time, it is important to take proactive steps to get your students actively involved in learning when they are in school.

Chapter

14

What to Do and How to Do it

1 Be clear about your perceptions of motivation.

Decide what motivation means to you.
The term "motivation" has different meanings for different people. One traditional definition describes motivation as providing an incentive, motive, or inducement. This definition could imply that teachers have a responsibility to provide students with interesting activities, praise for jobs well done, or incentives and reinforcers that generate student interest and participation. A second definition refers to motivation as a need or desire to do something. Thought of in this way, motivation is an internal process or state. This definition implies that motivation is an internal characteristic which may or may not be influenced by a teacher's behavior. These definitions present two different, but interesting, perspectives on motivation. Depending on their beliefs, some teachers work very hard at providing strong external motivators, while others prefer to focus on increasing students' internal motivation. We suggest that you use both approaches, and we hope that this chapter provides practical applications of each.

"Whatever is worth doing at all is worth doing well." Earl of Chesterfield

Remember how complicated the school environment can be. Motivating students is a complex undertaking. The factors related to each individual's level of motivation are unique and personal. There are many variables that impact student learning: The physical environment, psychosocial stressors, procedural requirements of school bureaucracies, instructional practices geared to large groups, and the personalities and characteristics of individual teachers. These, and other variables, interact to influence not only students' ability to learn, but also their interest in the learning process. No wonder the task of motivating large numbers of public school students is challenging for educators. Motivating students, especially those who are not intrinsically motivated, will likely require a variety of approaches and interventions. There is no one correct answer to the complicated question of how teachers can increase students' motivation to learn.

2 Begin by focusing on the basics.

Create an inviting learning environment.
Most of us have preferences related to our work environments. We know how we work best and where we feel most productive. Professional educators have recently begun to consider this fact and to place a higher priority on creating learning

- Use cheery, bright colors
- Change the decorations regularly
- Have lots of plants
- Regulate the temperature
- Make sure everyone has a seat and some space of his/her own
- Provide several different settings within your classroom (a reading center with an easy chair and soft lights, a quiet area for individual work, etc.)
- Post students' work in the classroom
- Create interesting displays on novel topics
- Make sure that drinking water is available and accessible
- Play soft music sometimes
- Keep your room clean and well-organized; cut down on clutter
- Greet your students at the door
- Bring animals into your classroom (fish, small animals, dog for a day, etc.)
- Change the seating arrangement from time to time
- Look at your room when you return after a weekend off, and ask yourself if it is warm and inviting

create a motivating learning environment

environments that are comfortable, pleasant, and stimulating. However, even if your school district has not yet responded to these initiatives, it is still possible to create an environment in your own classroom that is motivating for you and for your students. This box suggests some considerations for designing your teaching/learning environment.

Convey positive expectations. Teachers are very powerful figures. One of the strongest motivators for many students is a teaching style that conveys high expectations. In earlier chapters, we discussed ways to build a sense of community in your classroom, and strategies for communicating effectively. In addition to those considerations, we believe that it is important to consistently and continually show your students that you expect them to learn and to succeed. You can communicate your positive expectations clearly and directly, as well as through more subtle actions or words. One important approach is to model your own interest in learning and your own motivation to do the best you can. When students get the message that their teachers are bored, unenthusiastic, or uninterested, they are unlikely to maintain their own interest and enthusiasm. Let your students know that you have high expectations for them and that you believe learning is exciting, interesting, and enjoyable. Adopt the attitude of a coach—positive thinking can lead to success!

3 Pay attention to your interactions with students.

Be objective about the quality of your interactions. It is impossible to be both an observer of and a participant in a situation. When you are actively involved in teaching, you may not be aware of exactly what you are doing and saying, how often you do some things, and what effect your actions are having on your students. Without realizing their impact, we often use these commonplace activities to communicate our attitudes to our students:

- The types of questions we ask

- Whom we call on to answer questions and how often we call on them

- How long we wait for students to respond to a question or request

- The way we give corrective feedback

- The seating arrangement for students

- How often we provide opportunities for students to make choices and work independently

- The quality and tone of our personal interactions with students

These interactions usually occur so quickly and so frequently during the school day that it is difficult to recognize exactly what

we are doing. Start to monitor your own behavior. Examine the quality of your interactions with students. If necessary, ask a friend or mentor to visit your class, watch for a while, then share his/her observations with you. Recognize your behavior patterns with regard to the actions mentioned here. Keep track of the ways you communicate with your class as a whole, and with individual students.

Increase your positive, productive interactions. Once you are aware of your interaction patterns with students, there are several important strategies you can use to communicate high expectations to them. Some involve positive responses to students whose characteristics often predispose teachers to negative expectations. Other techniques focus on providing students with adequate opportunities for success. Here are some ideas that you may want to try:

- Keep low-achieving students with the group; don't always seat them in the back of the room away from the rest of the class.

- Call on all students, not just the ones who usually know the answer.

- Provide all students, not just the gifted ones, with challenging assignments.

- Praise all students frequently.

- Allow students adequate time to answer questions after you ask them. Give them a chance to think.

- Provide feedback that is clear and detailed, so that students know exactly what to do next time.

- Don't judge students on the basis of their race, gender, ethnic group, socio-economic status, siblings, appearance, etc. Make sure your interactions don't reflect different expectations on the basis of these characteristics.

- Avoid "lounge talk" that is really just gossip about students. Talking about students in the teachers' workroom can sometimes end up as a discussion of confidential information, derogatory or negative comments, or personal gripes. Keep your reflections professional and positive; set a good example for your peers.

● Stay open to student change; don't judge overall performance or limit your expectations on the basis of one or two assignments or a couple of test scores.

4 Develop a teaching style that works.

Examine your instructional style. One of the nice things about teaching is that each individual teacher is free to develop a teaching style that is unique. It is neither necessary nor desirable for all teachers to teach in the same way. However, educational research has identified and described some teaching practices that are clearly effective. While it is not always possible to determine precisely why they are effective, some are strongly related to students' motivation to learn. Form 67 is a simple checklist of teaching practices that are effective and are likely to increase the motivation of

Provide your students with choices. These can be simple, one-time opportunities, or more long-term options like:
- Let students select some of the teaching materials. They can suggest books, vote on authors, or contribute to topic selection.
- Design learning contracts with options, like "Do any three of these," or "For an A, do activities in sections 1, 2, and 3; for a B, complete 1 and 2 only."
- Allow students to choose between creating an original example of a concept, or writing a paper that describes the concept's historical background.

Allow students to make mistakes without ruining their grades.
- Give some assignments that are graded on the basis of completion only, especially when students are first learning material or beginning to practice.
- Allow students to correct mistakes and redo the assignment, then average the two scores.
- Give a grade based on the percentage of improvement a student demonstrates, but don't make this punishing for those who start out at high levels of achievement.

Use relevant materials.
- Use real life materials like newspapers, current music and literature, or examples from home and the community.
- Show your students why the material should be important to them.
- Invite older students and others from the community to share their experiences regarding the subject being taught.

Whenever possible, use a culminating activity that is hands-on and challenging.
- Get out your Bloom's Taxonomy list of cognitive skills. Design tasks that are at the highest levels (synthesis and evaluation), and require students to evaluate, critique, produce, etc.
- Let students work together. (We have discussed this in depth in Chapter 13.)
- Encourage students to seek resources for learning outside of school, in their communities.

Keep the pace of the class brisk.
- Make your teaching fast enough to keep students interested.
- Vary the activities. Design your lessons in short segments, and with a variety of direct instruction, questioning, discussion, group practice, and individual practice.
- Avoid wasting time. Keep interruptions to a minimum, and streamline your procedures for transitions.

Have fun!
- Do some things that are just for fun.
- Encourage and share humor.
- Laugh. It's good for the soul.

effective teaching practices to motivate students

even the most reluctant learners. Take a minute to examine your own teaching style, see how many of these practices you already use regularly, and decide which strategies you would like to initiate in the future.

Make your instruction more dynamic.
After you have completed the checklist on Form 67, you can decide which effective teaching practices you would like to implement or to use more often. First, review the information in Chapter 12 about individualizing instruction. One section of that chapter presents suggestions for different ways to teach the same material. This is an excellent way to start to modify your instruction: teach something in a new way. The box on the preceding page presents some other quick and easy ways to implement effective practices that are likely to motivate students.

"Laughter has no foreign accent."

Paul B. Lowney

---

5 Help students make the connection between effort and outcome.

Teach goal setting. One of the most powerful tools that individuals have is their own sense of efficacy: Their belief that what they do makes a difference. This belief is important not only for individual achievement

and motivation, but also because we are important role models for students. There's an old saying, "Concentrate on what you want." The point of this concept is twofold: If you stay focused mentally on your goal, and concentrate your efforts on reaching that goal, you will succeed. Discuss your own goals with your students, then teach your students to set some long-term and short-term goals (both academic and nonacademic) for themselves. Most of the inspirational and motivational speakers in our country today would add another step to the process: Write down your goals. Writing them down keeps them concrete, available, and real. Forms 68 and 69 are two tools to help your students articulate their own goals, and to motivate them to do what they must do to reach them.

Another strategy that motivational experts are in universal agreement about is making lists. Each day, make a list of what you want to accomplish. Cross off the things you complete, then move others to the top of the list. Do the same with a weekly and a monthly list of "Things to Do."

Expose your students to successful people and their ideas. Role models can have a profound impact on young people. Keep your students focused on positive people and positive ideas. Share your own successes with them. Let them meet everyday people who have positive attitudes, and

who have experienced success and reached high levels of achievement. You can bring in inspirational stories from the newspaper, video segments from television, magazine articles, and self-help books. Reinforce students for positive talk, and encourage them not to waste time blaming others and seeking excuses for their behavior. When people blame others, they are focusing on victimization and helplessness; encourage your students to create their own destinies. There is a wonderful little book called *Being Happy!* (Matthews, 1990). This book is quick and easy to read, entertaining, and full of practical ideas to share with your students. Start collecting resources like the *Being Happy!* book, so that you have plenty of tools to encourage and motivate your students.

Can't find anything that sparks that one particularly challenging student's excitement or

interest in school? Call home. Ask his/her mom, dad, brother, or sister. Find out what he/she likes to eat, ask about favorite television shows, and ask who his/her friends are. You may be surprised at some of the information you uncover.

6 Be creative.

Don't be afraid to use some "off-the-wall" approaches. Chapter 3 on positive reinforcement provided numerous suggestions and considerations for motivating students with extrinsic rewards. Review the basic principles of positive reinforcement, and develop a systematic plan for using the techniques mentioned. Remember, however, that what teachers consider reinforcing may not be reinforcing to students. It may be necessary to use approaches that are novel, surprising, or unexpected. People of all ages have stories to share about teachers who said and did things that were unusual, exciting, funny, or weird—all in order to motivate and excite their students. We have collected some ideas for approaches that are definitely not traditional, but can be highly motivating to students.

When you feel like giving up, don't.
Don't give up on the unmotivated students in your classes. When you feel tempted to

- Dress up. Use a costume related to a topic, or an outfit that fits a theme.
- Bring food. The fastest way to a student's head may really be through his/her stomach. Serve donuts and juice. Give them red-hots. Let them have chocolate-covered ants.
- Play funny games. Charades that fit vocabulary words are great. Use a Jeopardy!® format to ask comprehension questions. Play Trivial Pursuit®, or have a scavenger hunt.
- Use movement. Start your class with three minutes of exercise to music with an upbeat rhythm.
- Read aloud (and not from the textbook).
- Have a raffle for something great (like a CD or a concert ticket).
- Go places. Take a trip off campus. Go for a walk. Teach a unit that involves the outdoors.
- Have a Positive Thoughts Jar. Students and adults contribute their thoughts, then someone can read one each day.
- Post funny cartoons.
- Let them be the teachers. Take a day off, and let your students prepare and teach the lesson while you play the role of student.
- Have a singalong. Use a Karaoke®, or make a tape of the whole group.
- Teach them something different, like a card trick, an origami creation, or a phrase in a foreign language.

off-the-wall ways to motivate students

let them sleep in class, stop expecting them to make it, or write them off completely, try one more intervention, talk to them one more time, or share one more experience. Young people today face incredible pressures and overwhelming problems. You may be the only one who doesn't give up on a student, and you never know when something you say or do will "click." We've heard students say to teachers, "Well, I finally came around because you just wouldn't leave me alone. You wouldn't give up, so I decided not to give up." Hang in there!

"The time is always right to do what is right." *Martin Luther King, Jr.*

Forms
for
Chapter
14

form 67 Effective Teaching Practices: How Many of These Do You Use Regularly?

Rate yourself on these specific teaching behaviors. Then decide which one(s) you would like
to incorporate into your instruction.

Never = 1   Sometimes = 2   Always = 3

1. I provide all of my students with challenging activities. _____
2. When I teach, I provide my students with concrete examples. _____
3. I articulate and explain the objectives of lessons (or units). _____
4. I teach my students to set goals and to problem-solve. _____
5. I plan lessons that are novel, and I use a variety of approaches and activities. _____
6. The pace of my class is brisk. _____
7. I break tasks down into small steps. _____
8. I provide students with immediate feedback about their performance. _____
9. I give detailed, clear explanations. _____
10. I ask a lot of questions during instruction and I vary the types of questions. _____
11. I provide students with lots of practice on skills. _____
12. I am confident. _____
13. I minimize the time we waste on transitions. _____
14. I use games, fantasy, and/or simulations. _____
15. I allow a lot of peer interaction in my classroom. _____
16. I use suspense and encourage curiosity. _____
17. I structure all types of learning: Individual, competitive, and cooperative. _____
18. I modify and adapt tasks to fit individual students. _____
19. I refer to the value of academic activities and express my enthusiasm for learning. _____
20. I point out the relationship between effort and outcome. _____

(cont'd)

form 67 (cont'd)

Now, examine your responses:

1. Look at your total score. If your score is:

   50-60   You are above average in effective teaching skills
   40-49   You are inconsistent in applying effective teaching practices
   below 39 You need to improve your teaching skills

2. Circle those items that you rated with a 3 ("Always"). Congratulate yourself on using these effective techniques consistently.

3. Now, look at those items that you rated with a 2 ("Sometimes"). List them here.

   _____   _____

   _____   _____

   _____   _____

   Decide how you might become more consistent in implementing these strategies. What can you do to improve? Are there some ways of encouraging yourself? _____

   _____

4. Next, list the items that you rated with a 1 ("Never").

   _____   _____

   _____   _____

   _____   _____

   Do you know how to do these things? If not, who could help you learn? _____

   Which of these would be the easiest for you to implement? _____

   What materials do you need to help you begin to do these things? _____

   What are you going to do first? _____

form 68 Goal Setting and Adjustment

Goal Setting Form
Long-Term, Intermediate, or Short-Term? (circle one)

Personal/Social Goal	Vocational Goal	Academic Goal

Goal Reward Form

My goal is to:

_____

_____

By:

_____

If I make it, I will treat myself to:

_____

_____

Reprinted with permission from McCarron, L.T., Fad, K.M., & McCarron, M.B. (1992). *Achieving behavioral competencies: A program for developing social/emotional skills with secondary students.* Dallas, TX: McCarron-Dial Systems.

form 69 Goal Adjustment

Goal Adjustment Form
Original goal:
Problems with the goal:
Help you received from others:
Readjust your goal? How?
Give up your goal?

Reprinted with permission from McCarron, L.T., Fad, K.M., & McCarron, M.B. (1992). *Achieving behavioral competencies: A program for developing social/emotional skills with secondary students.* Dallas, TX: McCarron-Dial Systems.

help students generalize their skills

If we want students to be independent learners in all environments, we must teach them to maintain and generalize their skills.

It is important that students learn to monitor, evaluate, modify, reinforce, and maintain skills themselves, without constant supervision or guidance from teachers. Only then will they succeed as independent, productive adults.

Chapter 15

What to Do and How to Do it

1 Emphasize the importance of self-management.

Teach students why they should control their own behavior. There are several reasons students should begin to monitor and regulate their own behavior. First, adults will not always be close to or actively involved in students' daily activities. This is increasingly true as a student grows older and more independent. Adolescents and young adults will (and should) have opportunities to go places, do things, and make decisions without adult supervision. Second, as young people take steps toward independence, they will not only have freedom, but they will also be held accountable for the decisions they make. While young children are likely to be forgiven for some poor choices because of their immaturity, older children are increasingly responsible for their own behavior. Third, it is important that students develop a sense that they control what happens to them. This internal locus of control is a vital component of independent achievement. Without it, students may get stuck in patterns of blaming others for their own failures or problems. They may also lack the initiative necessary to succeed in the workplace and in relationships. In talking with your students, discuss the importance of self-reliance, independence, and self-control as strategies that will lead to greater happiness and success.

Encourage students to begin to think for themselves. In education, there is a body of research related to the teaching of thinking. This research suggests that people behave as they do not just because of external rules, but also because of the internal model of the world they create for themselves. In effect, what people do is create a very personal vision (or model) of how the world works. As our lives unfold, we test what happens to us against our model of how we think the world should work. When things go as we expect them to, it confirms our belief in our model; when situations go awry, we may alter our internal model.

When teachers or parents rely solely on external factors like rules, consequences, and positive reinforcement to control students' behavior, it may limit students' opportunities to use their personal experiences to create their own model of how the world works. We see this with students who behave well only when closely supervised or who succeed only in highly structured situations. If we want students to function well independently and make good decisions on their own, we must teach them to use their experiences to develop a positive model of how the world works. As students are supported in their learning of skills like problem solving and self-control, they develop a framework for making good choices. When a new challenge arises that they must face alone, students can remember their past experiences. They can use their positive model of how and why the world works, apply their knowledge to the new situation, and make a good decision *without* relying on an adult.

"To think is easy. To act is difficult. To act as one thinks is the most difficult of all." Johann Wolfgang von Goethe

---

2 Teach students to recognize what they are doing.

Improve their self-assessment skills.

Many students do not realize what they do, how often they do it, how it looks to others, and what impact it has on others in their environment. Not only do students who have emotional or attention/hyperactivity disorders fail to recognize and control their own behaviors, sometimes average or highly gifted students also lack these important abilities. Before students can control their behavior, they must realize what they are actually doing. You can help students become objective observers of themselves in several ways. Try some of these ideas for teaching students to become accurate in assessing their own behaviors:

- Begin with general self-ratings.

  Using self-ratings can help students begin to look at how they feel and how they act. A rating tool like Form 70 focuses on general, broad behaviors. This type of self-rating asks students to evaluate their long-term overall functioning, and is useful with students who have little or no awareness of themselves.

- Use more specific self-evaluations.

  As students mature and learn rules and positive social skills, self-assessment can shift to more specific behaviors.

An example of a more specific self-evaluation is the one shown on Form 71. With this type of evaluation, students reflect on their performance of particular skills.

- Use mediation questionnaires or essays.

  Sometimes, evaluating behavior is more complicated. When students are highly emotional, impulsive, or reactive, their emotional state interferes with their ability to make decisions and control their behavior. When this happens consistently, their self-evaluations may need to be more reflective. In these cases, asking students to elaborate on their feelings is important. Find out how the student was feeling at the time of a particular incident, why the student did what he/she did, and what the response was to the student's behavior. Then you can help the student to choose other, more beneficial responses in the future. Form 53 in Chapter 10 is a nice example of a mediation essay form that calls for short responses.

Encourage them to monitor frequencies of behavior.
One of the most effective ways to help students realistically assess their skills and progress (both academic and social) is to teach them to count specific behaviors. Using a simple tally sheet like Form 72 is the quickest and easiest way to do this. After the student has identified and

described a target behavior, turn over the job of counting to him/her. Choose one of the tally sheets on the form and show your student how to use it. The method is most effective if you can be very specific about the behavior you want the student to count. Define the behavior clearly and make sure you both agree on what counts and what doesn't.

For example, if Megan is constantly complaining, ask her to make a tally mark for each negative comment she makes. If Joe never seems to complete his work because he always "feels sick," ask him to record each health complaint. After a week, you can help him evaluate how serious a problem he has and whether his complaints are more frequent during particular class periods, on certain days, or in conjunction with other events.

3 Provide students with ways to check their perceptions.

Teach them to do some "reality checks." In any situation in which two or more people interact, the individuals involved are likely to form very different impressions of what is happening. Because each person has his/her own point of view, their perceptions are likely to differ. Often, our perceptions are influenced by our emotional state, our prior history with specific people, our goals, and numerous other factors.

Consequently, our perceptions of ourselves and others may not always be accurate. Occasionally, we all need a little reality check to see if what we think is happening is, in fact, happening. Here are several strategies to help your students compare their own perceptions and impressions with those held by others:

● Use videotape.

Videotaping students during social skills lessons, regular class activities, and other situations during the school day can be a great teaching tool. After the taping, set aside time so that students can review their behavior with you. Stop the action, discuss what's going on, and help them reflect on what you see and what they see. Use lots of processing questions like, "What did you mean by . . . ?"; "How do you think the others felt when . . . ?"; "How could you

have said that differently?"; and "Why did you . . . ?"

● Teach them to compare their impressions with actual performance.

If your students have daily contracts, report cards, punch cards, or other behavior monitoring forms, use them to provide data for comparisons. Students can check their progress by answering questions like the ones on Form 73.

● Use social skills curricula to build high-level skills.

Most of the social skills curricula available today include topics such as demonstrating sensitivity, expressing empathy, active listening (including how to pick up on non-verbal cues), and how to accept criticism and feedback. Use these curricula to foster students' awareness of how other people perceive them. As students master these high-level skills, they should become more adept at accurately assessing what others think of them, so that they are clear about why they receive the reactions they do from others.

● Use a "Whirlpool."

Students can give each other useful feedback that helps them stay reality-based. One way to structure positive group feedback is to use a Whirlpool. In this process, one student sits in front of a small semicircle of three to five peers. The student can ask his/her peers questions about his/her behavior, or peers can offer comments and suggestions. It is important that you not allow the Whirlpool to become a negative situation in which students "gang up" on the person in the middle. Feedback should describe behaviors, not make judgments, so each participant should be required to offer at least one positive or constructive comment.

Be honest. Most educators are sensitive, caring people. When teachers interact with students, they do not want to hurt feelings, damage self-esteem, discourage, or disappoint. Teachers also have empathy and understanding for students who have physical, emotional, or cognitive disorders; are abused or neglected at home; or whose prior experiences in school have been negative. Consequently, teachers may sometimes be overly sensitive, understanding, or caring. They may overlook or tolerate behaviors that will not be overlooked in the "real world." You are not doing your students a favor if you allow them to persist in behaviors that are unproductive or disruptive. In the world of work, families, and friends, people must be honest with themselves about what they are doing, what impact their behavior has on others, and how they measure up to the standards set for

---

Teaching Students to Self-Reinforce:

- Put students in charge of their own rewards.

  If you use a token economy or other reward system with students, begin to turn over the monitoring and reinforcement to them. Allow them to take tokens when they meet criteria, record points if they have followed the rules, and "pay" themselves when they complete their tasks.

- Teach them to visualize. Visualizing themselves doing well helps students develop a belief that they can achieve their goals. They can also visualize the positive outcomes for achieving the goals. When students don't have many positive role models in real life, this helps them to become, in effect, their own models.

  Teach your students to visualize themselves engaging in a positive behavior, then visualize themselves in a positive situation as a reward (listening to a compliment, getting a good grade, earning a privilege, etc.). Visualization techniques can be learned even by young children. (Like any other skill, though, they must be practiced in order to remain effective.)

- Teach students the art of self-talk.

  For students who have not experienced a lot of success, the idea of reinforcing themselves may seem artificial, phony, or awkward. They may need to learn some words to say to themselves (a script) when they have succeeded at something. Teach them to give themselves pep talks like, "That was great! I stuck with it until I reached my goal," or "Nice job, Dion, you're really on a roll now." Keep the scripts short, positive, and realistic.

teach them to rely on themselves

---

them. Being honest with your students and teaching them to be honest with themselves will help them succeed in the future.

"We are what we pretend to be, so we must be careful about what we pretend to be."   *Kurt Vonnegut*

4 Teach students to reinforce themselves.

Consider the importance of self-reinforcement. The source of most positive reinforcement is external. Teachers usually control the distribution of it, making decisions about what reinforcers to use, how often to use them, what the specific contingencies will be, and when to stop reinforcing students. When teachers are systematic, consistent, and creative, positive reinforcement strategies work well, and many educators endorse their use enthusiastically. On the other hand, there are also many critics of positive reinforcement. These professionals view positive reinforcement as ineffective, limited in scope, and/or unlikely to result in lasting changes in behavior. They encourage teachers to foster intrinsic motivation in students instead of using extrinsic rewards. We believe that both approaches have merit, and that as you use external positive reinforcers, you should also teach students how to reinforce and motivate themselves. Students must not continue to rely on others to make them feel good about their accomplishments, to reward them for a job well done, or to give them a pat on the back when they reach a goal.

Teach them some basic self-reinforcement techniques. In Chapter 8, we introduced the use of the Am I Working?

technique (Form 43). This strategy helps students monitor themselves for on-task behavior. If you teach your students to follow up by reinforcing themselves, they become their own teachers. In the box on the previous page are several other strategies that will help you begin to teach students to reinforce themselves.

5 Teach students to monitor their progress.

Let them take responsibility for record keeping. One excellent strategy for helping students become better at controlling their own behavior is to teach them to recognize and record their progress. Students often lose sight of the big picture; that is, they are not realistic about their long-term patterns of behavior and their progress toward goals. A visual representation, like a graph or chart, can be a big help to students. Try using a chart like Form 74. A student can use this form to plot his/her attendance percentage for about a month. The student can

immediately interpret the information to find out whether his/her attendance follows a pattern, exactly when problems begin to arise, or how much of an impact his/her attendance may be having on academic performance.

Encourage independence. It is often difficult for teachers to "let go" of students. Along with independence comes the opportunity to get hurt or to fail. Nevertheless, you must allow students the "dignity of risk," encouraging them to take appropriate risks and to determine their own destinies. Teach them the skills they need to be independent, then let them go.

Forms
for
Chapter
15

form 70 Improving Self-Awareness

Circle the number that best describes you for each of these items. Try to be as honest as you can.

	5	4	3	2	1
1. I am even-tempered					I get mad easily
2. I am usually happy	5	4	3	2	1 I am usually sad
3. I can do most things asked of me	5	4	3	2	1 I can't do most things asked of me
4. I have confidence in myself	5	4	3	2	1 I have no confidence in myself
5. I care for people	5	4	3	2	1 I do not care for people
6. I am fun to be with	5	4	3	2	1 I am not fun to be with
7. I am strong	5	4	3	2	1 I am weak
8. I am healthy	5	4	3	2	1 I am not healthy
9. I like to play	5	4	3	2	1 I don't like to play
10. I like to work	5	4	3	2	1 I don't like to work
11. I get my work done	5	4	3	2	1 I don't finish my work
12. I like myself	5	4	3	2	1 I don't like myself

Reprinted with permission from McCarron, L.T., Fad, K.M., & McCarron, M.B. (1992).
Achieving behavioral competencies: A program for developing social/emotional skills with secondary students. Dallas, TX: McCarron-Dial Systems.

form 71 Sensitivity Self-Evaluation

1. Do my friends seem to talk to me about their personal problems or achievements?

2. Do I listen well to others? Do I spend more time talking, or listening?

3. Can I understand how others feel?

4. Do I give too much advice?

5. Do I always have a situation of my own to talk about instead of just listening?

6. Can I pick up on feelings by watching body language, tone of voice, facial expressions, etc.?

7. Do I change my behavior when I can tell that a friend is upset, angry, sad, happy, etc.?

8. Does it seem like people trust me with their feelings?

9. Do I feel comfortable when someone confides in me?

10. Do people say that I'm a good listener or a good friend?

Reprinted with permission from McCarron, L.T., Fad, K.M., & McCarron, M.B. (1992).
Achieving behavioral competencies: A program for developing social/emotional skills with secondary students. Dallas, TX: Mc-Carron-Dial Systems.

form 72 Tally Sheet

Behavior Tally Sheet

I am going to count how many times I:

_____

_____

I will count this behavior from _____ until _____.

Here are the tally marks:

Behavior Counting Sheet

I am going to count how many times I:

_____

_____

I will count this behavior from _____ until _____.

Each number circled indicates an occurrence of the behavior.

1	2	3	4	5	6	7	8	9	10
11	12	13	14	15	16	17	18	19	20
21	22	23	24	25	26	27	28	29	30
31	32	33	34	35	36	37	38	39	40
41	42	43	44	45	46	47	48	49	50

form 73 Double-Checking My Progress

In reviewing my progress, I have noticed the following about my behavior:

1. I did well on: _____

   _____

   _____

2. The consequences for my good behavior were: _____

   _____

   _____

3. I did/did not reach my goals for last week. (If not, complete # 4.)_____

   _____

   _____

4. The reasons I did not reach my goals last week are: _____

   _____

   _____

5. For next week, my goals are:_____

   _____

   _____

6. To reach them, I am going to:_____

   _____

   _____

form 74 Individual Attendance Record

Each school day, compute your attendance percentage by dividing the number of classes you attended by the number of classes in the school day. Then mark the appropriate box on this graph.

Student: _____ Month of: _____

Attendance (Percentage of Classes Attended)

100
95
90
85
80
75
70
65
60
55
50
45
40
35
30
25
20

Dates

references

Algozzine, R. (1993, February). *Working with students who are seriously emotionally disturbed*. Presentation at the Behavioral Disorders Conference, Austin, TX.

Black, D.B., Downs, J., Bastien, J., Brown, L.J., & Wells, P. (1987). *Social skills in the school*. Boys Town, NE: Division of Education, Father Flanagan's Boys' Home.

Bloom, B.S., Englehart, N.D., Furst, E.J., Hill, W.H., & Krathwohl, D.R. (1956). *Taxonomy of educational objectives: The classification of educational goals: Handbook I: Cognitive domain*. New York: McKay.

Choate, J.S. (Ed.) (1993). *Successful mainstreaming: Proven ways to detect and correct special needs*. Boston: Allyn and Bacon.

Colvin, G. & Sugai, G. (1989). *Managing escalating behavior*. Eugene, OR: Behavior Associates.

Crisis Intervention Training:
National Crisis Prevention Institute
3315-K North 124th Street
Brookfield, Wisconsin 53005
1-800-558-8976
1-414-783-5787

Gilliam, J.E. & McConnell, K.S. (1996). *Scales for predicting successful inclusion*. Austin, TX: Pro-Ed.

Goldstein, A.P. & Glick, B. (1987). *Aggression replacement training*. Champaign, IL: Research Press.

Great Falls Public Schools. (1993). *Project RIDE: Responding to individual differences in education (Elementary version)*. Longmont, CO: Sopris West.

Huggins, P. (1991). *Creating a caring classroom*. Longmont, CO: Sopris West.

Huggins, P. (1991). *Helping kids handle anger*. Longmont, CO: Sopris West.

Jenson, W.R., Rhode, G., & Reavis, H.K. (1994). *The tough kid tool box*. Longmont, CO: Sopris West.

Matthews, A. (1990). *Being happy!* Los Angeles, CA: Price Stern Sloan.

McCarron, L.T., Fad, K.M., & McCarron, M.B. (1992). *Achieving behavioral competencies: A program for developing social/emotional skills with secondary students*. Dallas, TX: McCarron-Dial Systems.

McGinnis, E. & Goldstein, A.P. (1984). *Skillstreaming the elementary school child*. Champaign, IL: Research Press.

Murphy, D.A., Meyers, C.C., Olesen, S., McKean, K., & Custer, S.H. (1995). *Exceptions: A handbook of inclusion activities for teachers of students at grades 6-12 with mild disabilities* (2nd ed.). Longmont, CO: Sopris West.

Rhode, G., Jenson, W.R., & Reavis, H.K. (1992). *The tough kid book: Practical classroom management strategies*. Longmont, CO: Sopris West.

Sprick, R., Sprick, M., & Garrison, M. (1993). *Interventions: Collaborative planning for students at risk*. Longmont, CO: Sopris West.

Wood, J.W. (1993). *Mainstreaming: A practical approach for teachers* (2nd ed.). New York: Merrill.

recommended resources

Ashton, M. & Varga, L. (1993). *101 games for groups.* Tucson, AZ: Communication Skill Builders.

Gardner, M. (1988). *Perplexing puzzles and tantalizing teasers.* New York: Dover Publications.

Jackson, T. (1993). *Activities that teach.* Cedar City, UT: Red Rock Publishing.

Matthews, A. (1991). *Making friends.* Los Angeles: Price Stern Sloan.

Polloway, E.A. & Patton, J.R. (1993). *Strategies for teaching learners with special needs (5th ed.).* New York: Macmillan.

Rubin, D. (1988). *Brainstorms: Real puzzles for the real genius.* New York: Harper & Row.

Seaman, J. (1996). *Teaching kids to learn: An integrated study skills curriculum for grades 5-7.* Longmont, CO: Sopris West.

Sushan, R. (Ed.). (1984). *Games Magazine big book of games.* New York: Workman Publishing.

Social Skills

Brown, L., Black, D., & Downs, J. (1984). *School social skills rating scale.* East Aurora, NY: Slosson Educational Publications.

Goldstein, A.P., Sprafkin, R.P., Gershaw, N.J., & Klein, P. (1980). *Skillstreaming the adolescent.* Champaign, IL: Research Press.

Hazel, J.S., Schumaker, J.B., Sherman, J.A., & Sheldon-Wildgen, J. (1981). *ASSET: A social skills program for adolescents.* Champaign, IL: Research Press.

Jackson, N.F., Jackson, D.A., & Monroe, C. (1983). *Getting along with others: Teaching social effectiveness to children.* Champaign, IL: Research Press.

Utah State University, Department of Special Education. (1982). *Teaching social skills to handicapped youth: Programs and materials.* Logan, UT: Author.

Waksman, S. (1984). *Waksman social skills rating scale.* Portland, OR: ASIEP Education.

Walker, H., McConnell, S., Holmes, D., Todis, B., Walker, J., & Golden, N. (1983). *The Walker social skills curriculum: The ACCEPTS program.* Austin, TX: Pro-Ed.

Cooperative Learning

Aronson, E., Blaney, N., Stephan, C., Sikes, J., & Snapps, M. (1978). *The jigsaw classroom.* Newbury Park, CA: SAGE Publications.

Baratta-Lorton, M. (1976). *Mathematics their way.* Menlo Park, CA: Addison-Wesley.

Bellanca, J. & Fogarty, R. (1990). *Blueprints for thinking in the cooperative classroom.* Palatine, IL: Skylight.

Burns, M. (1977). *The good times math event book.* Oak Lawn, IL: Creative Publications.

Cohen, E.G., (1986). *Designing groupwork: Strategies for the heterogeneous classroom.* New York: Teachers College Press.

DeAvila, E.A., Duncan, S.E., & Navarette, C.J. (1986). Finding out/Descubrimiento. Northvale, NJ: Santilla.

Dishon, D. & O'Leary, P.W. (1984). *A guidebook for cooperative learning: A technique for creating more effective schools.* Holmes Beach, FL: Learning Publications.

Glasser, W. (1986). *Control theory in the classroom.* New York: Harper and Row.

Johnson, D.W. & Johnson, R.T. (1987). *Learning together and alone: Cooperative, competitive, and individualistic Learning* (2nd ed.). Englewood Cliffs, NJ: Prentice Hall.

Johnson, R. & Johnson D. (1986). *Circles of learning: Cooperation in the classroom.* Alexandria, VA: Association of Supervisors and Curriculum Directors.

Kagan, S. (1988). *Cooperative learning: Research for teachers.* Riverside, CA: University of California.

Kohn, A. (1986). *No Contest: The case against competition.* Boston: Houghton Mifflin.

Male, M., Johnson, D.W., & Johnson, R.T. (1986). *Cooperative learning and computers: An activity guide for teachers* (3rd ed.). Santa Cruz, CA: Educational Apple-cations.

Sharan, S. and Sharan, Y. (1976). *Small group teaching.* Englewood Cliffs, NJ: Educational Testing Publications.

Sharan, S., Hare, P., Webb, C., & Hertz-Lazarowitz, R. (Eds.). (1980). *Cooperation in Education.* Provo, UT: Brigham Young University Press.

Slavin, R.E. (1986). *Using student team learning* (3rd ed.). Baltimore, MD: Center for Research on Elementary and Middle Schools, The Johns Hopkins University.

Slavin, R.E. (1983). *Cooperative learning.* New York: Longman.